Haynes

Build your own
Gaming PC

Published by: Haynes Publishing
Sparkford, Yeovil, Somerset BA22 7JJ, UK
Tel: 01963 442030 Fax: 01963 440001
Int. tel: +44 1963 442030 Fax: +44 1963 440001
E-mail: sales@haynes.co.uk
Website: www.haynes.co.uk

British Library Cataloguing in Publication Data:
A catalogue record for this book is available from the British Library

ISBN 978 0 85733 802 0

Library of Congress control no. 2014957830

Printed in the USA by Odcombe Press LP,
1299 Bridgestone Parkway, La Vergne, TN 37086

Haynes

Build your own
Gaming PC

Russell Barnes and Adam Barnes

Contents

1

PART  Why build your own gaming PC?

With so many amazing options available to buy ready-made gaming PCs from brilliant makers like Chillblast.com and Overclockers.co.uk you may wonder why anyone would want to build their own gaming PC at all. After all, there's bound to be a system that suits your needs among the hundreds available, and that shiny new PC could be on your doorstep within 48 hours.

The answers are simple: choice, budget and upgradability. You have the opportunity to create an entirely custom PC designed specifically with your needs in mind and, regardless of what the marketing men would have you believe, you're the only one that can deliver it.

As you might already know, high-end gaming hardware tends to be more expensive than the average run-of-the-mill kit, so (like it or not) your available budget is going to play a very key role in the end result. The most important parts of the puzzle also tend to be the most expensive. The Central Processing Unit (CPU) and Graphics Processing Unit (GPU), or graphics card, are where a good third of your entire budget is going to be spent.

PART  Bang for buck

Finding that elusive but oh-so-important sweet spot between performance and price isn't easy but certainly worth the trouble investigating. Most high-end gaming PC manufacturers don't really want you to know it (and console makers like Sony and Microsoft definitely don't), but you don't have to spend the equivalent of six months' wages to get the most out of today's hottest games.

NVIDIA's new Titan X GPU is mightily impressive – it's like having a GTX 980 and GTX 960 strapped on one card – yet it costs much more than those two cards combined.

If all you had to do to build the perfect gaming PC was to buy the most expensive components on the market, the process would be child's play. It would also bankrupt the best of us. Besides, while you'd probably succeed in building a pretty impressive machine, and receive all the bragging rights that come with it, you would have wasted a lot of money for very little gain. You see one of the most important lessons you learn from shopping smart is that an extra 25% on the price simply doesn't equate to an extra 25% in performance. In fact, beyond a certain threshold it's not even close.

Spending £5,000 on a gaming PC is easy, but spending 100% more for barely 10% more performance is just plain foolish. That's pretty shocking in itself, but when you consider what that extra 10% of performance actually represents you'll be

even more disappointed. Our target is to play the hottest games at full graphical fidelity at a smooth and steady 60 frames per second (FPS) – an extra 10% here would equate to an extra 6 FPS.

The higher you get up towards the most prestigious of the high-end components, the bigger the disparity between price and performance too. To cut a long story short, buying smart isn't buying the very latest kit; in fact, some of the smartest purchases might not even be from the very latest hardware generation.

So we don't have to spend a fortune, but we still need a degree in electronic engineering, right? Actually, no. Modern computer hardware is incredibly user-friendly, making it more like a super-charged LEGO set than anything else. You can choose from an ever-growing pool of components to slot together your perfect PC within a couple of hours. The level of overall compatibility component-to-component is actually incredibly high, and modern motherboards (the backbone of any computer) are so complete and self-contained that the process isn't far off being plug-and-play.

All it takes is a little bit of informed courage, giving you enough information to roll up your sleeves and get started, and that's what this book is all about.

It might be scary to look at, but with the necessary information you'll find you have no problem installing any part of a PC; it's actually pretty simple, these days.

PART  Understanding your needs

When it comes to building a gaming PC you first need to ask yourself what it is you want to get out of the machine. High-end PC games can require a great deal of computing power to run at their very best, but that doesn't mean you need to spend over the odds for an enjoyable gaming experience. As already mentioned, your budget will play a great deal in what sort of PC you can build, but you should also think about the types of games you're interested in playing, whether you'll be transporting it around for regular LAN events or even where you'll be keeping it – you don't want an ugly PC case if it's to sit opposite your living-room TV, after all. We've detailed some of the types of machines you might want to aim for and the kinds of parts you'll want to buy; and don't worry, we'll explain the hardware in closer detail later.

PC gaming is home to some of the biggest, most impressive looking titles. If you want the very best gaming can offer, you'll need a gaming PC.

A high-end gaming PC will always outperform the consoles in terms of graphical prowess, and there are companies – such as Crytek – who relish in making the best-looking games possible.

£500 low-end gaming PC

Many are surprised to hear just how low cost a gaming PC can be, and in truth the savviest of buyers will be able to get a full gaming PC for even less than £500. There are concessions, of course. With a build like this you will be going for more generic parts, and while that's not often an issue you should – as always – remember that old adage, 'you get what you pay for'. That's not to say you can't build a suitable and functional gaming PC at this price range, but you do need to pay closer attention to reviews to ensure your cheap parts aren't cheaply made.

It does mean that you won't ever see high-end games at their very best, either. You'll still be able to run the majority of your games well – in most cases even on 'High' settings – but in this price range you're looking at a system that will age much quicker since you're already coming in at the low-end. If you're on a budget – or are simply looking to play those inventive 2D indie games that don't come over to consoles – then this is the rig for you.

Ultimately you'll be cutting costs primarily with lower-spec CPUs and graphics cards, the latter of which will primarily affect just which games you can play – and how well those you can play will actually look. Here's an example of a low-end £500 PC build:

- Cooler Master K350 Mid-Tower Case
- Asus H81M-Plus Intel H81 Chipset Motherboard
- Intel Pentium G3240 3.1GHz Dual Core CPU
- EVGA GTX 750 Ti 2GB GPU
- Corsair Vengeance 1600MHz 8GB RAM
- Seagate 7200rpm 1TB HDD
- Corsair VS550 PSU

£800 mid-range gaming PC

At this price you're more in the range of a gaming PC that could last you for a handful of years without ever the need to upgrade. It will handle practically everything you throw at it, and though you might not be able to play every game on its 'Ultra' settings you can rest easy knowing that the visual upgrade won't be all that dissimilar to your own. In fact, this is perhaps the best range to aim for – at least initially – since you'll have a comfortable gaming experience without having to worry too heavily about all the extra bits and pieces you can bundle in there.

Additionally, you can aim for this price range for a more portable PC, perhaps for one you'd like to take to a friend's house, or use when attending LAN events. The case will be important in this situation, and as a result so will the parts you can fit in. Be careful when buying Micro PC cases; there are a lot more stipulations in the parts you can get.

All the same, whether you're aiming for a standard desktop or something more portable, at this price you're going to get a machine that runs everything quite comfortably at 1080p and 60 frames per second. Here's an example of a smaller form factor gaming PC build:

- Bitfenix Prodigy Case
- Asus Z97I-Plus Motherboard
- Intel Core i5 4690K
- Arctic Cooling Freezer 7 Pro Rev 2 CPU cooler
- NVIDIA GeForce GTX 960 2GB
- 8GB PC3-12800 DDR3 Memory
- 1TB Seagate SSHD Hybrid drive
- Corsair CX600 PSU

£1400 high-end gaming PC

Make no mistake, this is by no means the top echelon of gaming PCs, but in terms of horsepower this price range offers no-holds-barred, high-end gaming with a full range of extras. Here you're looking at techy additions such as solid-state drives, water cooling and the capacity for Scalable Link Interface (SLI) graphics cards. Don't worry if you don't know what all that means; that's why we're here. If you want the absolute best, then roughly around this price range – give or take a couple of hundred – will get you exactly that without any future concerns.

It's the extra features that really make a build like this, however. Water cooling might sound risky for an electronic device, but it offers up a silent alternative to traditional fan

cooling – which is especially important when including so many top-end, power-hungry parts that like to run hot. A solid-state drive (SSD) is a different type of hard drive, one that can read and write data exceptionally quickly – and therefore load your games and even your operating system much quicker than your typical drives. It's in extras like this that you can really build a gaming PC that can run games at their very best *and* provide as smooth a user experience as possible to whoever might use it.

It'll also take a good few years before the inevitable depreciation of hardware begins to set in; if you want a machine that you won't need to adjust, upgrade or replace for many, many years then look to this price range. Here's an example of a high-end gaming PC build:

Indie gaming is particularly popular on PC due to the ease with which games can be published on the platform. Often these games begin as exclusive to the platform, or are available much cheaper.

- NZXT Source 340 Mid-Tower Case
- Gigabyte X99 Gaming 5 Motherboard
- Intel Haswell-E 5820K 3.30GHz CPU
- Corsair H100i water cooler
- MSI GeForce GTX 970 4GB
- Crucial PC4-17000 CL16 16GB DDR4 RAM
- Samsung 840 EVO 2.5in 250GB SSD
- Seagate 2TB SSHD 3.5in Hard Drive
- Corsair CX750 PSU

> HAUL: £841
> BANK: £2678

> TOOL: NONE

rrent Property: 253, Cyber Alley

PART **1** The tools of the trade

Since most modern computer components snap together more like elaborate LEGO for grown-ups than precision electronic components, you really don't need to have anything particularly special to hand to help you build your gaming PC. That said, there are a handful of items and considerations to keep in mind.

Anti-static

There are a few hurdles and stumbling blocks to bear in mind. The first of which is any electronic device's nemesis: static electricity. Is it possible to kill a £450 graphics card simply by taking it out of its anti-static bag? Yes, absolutely, and it really can happen. Before you handle any of your gaming PC's prized components you should ground yourself. The briefest touch of the nearest radiator or pipework will do the trick provided you're not then scuffing your feet back along nylon carpet to your workbench. Another solution is to use an anti-static wristband. It'll help stop the natural build-up of static electricity but is far from a requirement.

Cable ties

Something you'll hear quite a lot about as we guide you through the process of building your own PC in this book is airflow and the need to keep your computer as cool as possible. Heat is your enemy. It shortens the lives of your components and it makes for a noisier PC (more fans working harder to

keep temperatures down). One of the easiest ways to help keep temperatures down inside your PC is to ensure that the flow of air through your case from the front, or top, to the rear 'exhaust' of your PC is free from the jumble of cables inside your case. The easiest way to tame this tangle is with some carefully placed cable ties. They're very cheap and disposable – you don't have to use them sparingly.

Phillips screwdriver

Last, but certainly not least, is the humble Phillips screwdriver. Believe it or not, this is the only tool you need (though it doesn't hurt to have a small pair of long-nosed pliers to hand). The beauty of most modern gaming cases is the fact that they offer almost completely tool-less construction. Almost everything can be slotted or clipped or screwed (and even then most screws are thumbscrews, meaning they can be done by hand).

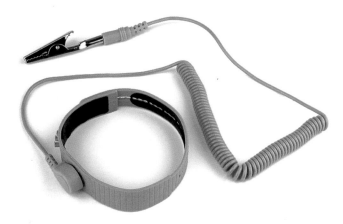

Installing software

You may notice that we haven't included a DVD (optical) drive in any of our builds. That's largely because no one involved in the making of this book has touched a DVD or compact disc of any kind in the last three years. We appreciate that might not apply to everyone and some readers might wonder how they're supposed to install Windows or a Linux distribution like Ubuntu or Steam OS.

For Windows you simply need to download an official ISO (disk image) from Microsoft and their handy USB tool, which you can find at http://windows.microsoft.com/en-GB/windows-8/create-reset-refresh-media. All you need is an 8GB USB stick.

Now that Steam OS, the Linux-based operating system powering Steam Machines, has over 1,000 supported games you might want to give that a try. For full instructions for installing it via a USB stick just visit http://store.steampowered.com/steamos.

PART  Anatomy of a gaming PC

On the face of it, building your own gaming PC sounds like a difficult and complicated task that could turn into an engineering marathon. While it is certainly true that you can spend months building a modified case with a custom liquid-cooling system, it is also possible to slap the hardware together in less than an hour.

Perhaps that sounds impossible so let's walk through the steps:

Open the case, install the power supply, install a motherboard with CPU, memory and cooler, plug in a graphics card, add an SSD or hard drive and then install Windows. If you're building a conventional PC and work methodically it is quite easy to assemble the hardware in less time than it takes to install Windows and the gigabytes of Windows Updates that are inevitably required. But let's be realistic. This isn't a sprint to the line and neither is it a marathon. If this is your first PC build and you have all the necessary parts to hand then you can be confident of starting the job after breakfast and having your first online death match underway by mid-afternoon.

On the other hand, if you plan the job poorly, you may spend some time shopping for a power supply extension cable or a cooling fan that is essential to finish the job. We should also sound a note of caution: if you order incompatible parts (such as the wrong memory or processor), you may find yourself in the position where it is impossible to complete your PC build without ordering a replacement component.

PART **2**

ANATOMY OF A GAMING PC

Understanding the basics

Let's start at the beginning with a list of components. If you dismantle pretty much any PC you will end up with a motherboard, processor, memory, graphics, cooling, SSD/hard drive, case and power supply. While it is also common to find a DVD drive this is not strictly necessary and these days networking and audio are likely to be features that are integrated as part of the motherboard where once they would have been separate expansion cards.

You will often hear a particular component called by different names so a mainboard is the same thing as a motherboard, a graphics card is a VGA (Video Graphics Adapter), a case is an enclosure and RAM (Random Access Memory) is also called system memory.

NVIDIA GTX Titan is based on a design used to power supercomputers. Utterly bonkers, completely over the top and highly desirable.

Even popular strategy games like *Civilization V* can be surprisingly demanding on your computer. Adjusting the game's settings will help it run more in tune with your computer.

There is no escaping the fact that the computer industry loves acronyms. In addition to VGA and RAM, you will doubtless come across CPU (Central Processing Unit), PSU (Power Supply Unit), HDD (Hard Disk Drive), SSD (Solid State Drive) and many more. You do not necessarily need to understand what each and every acronym means, but once in a while you need to stop and double-check the alphabet soup isn't leading you astray. It is all too easy to look at a graphics card with DVI-I and HDMI outputs (they are different types of connections for displays and TVs) and note that your intended 4K display also has HDMI and think 'Yes, that works, I just need an HDMI cable.'

And you'd be correct; it would display a picture. However, many 4K displays run at 60Hz refresh rate over HDMI while a tiny number are limited to 30Hz over HDMI and require DisplayPort for 60Hz. In other words, you will be able to connect the monitor to your graphics card, but they very possibly won't work well enough together to play games with the image quality you likely expect.

We will be covering peripherals (including displays) in Chapter 5 – this is merely an illustration that hardware that connects together does not necessarily work correctly. The only way around this conundrum is a decent amount of research. First you need to arrive at an approximate specification for your new gaming PC, which will give you an indication of the budget you need to spend, and then you can narrow down the selection to arrive at specific makes and models of hardware.

Five or ten years ago you could grab the DVD case of the latest version of *Battlefield*, or any other mainstream game, and see how the minimum and recommended system requirements compared to your own PC. 'Minimum system requirements' means the hardware that will play the game at medium to low settings while 'recommended' should work well with every quality setting at the maximum. In the past this basically meant you bought the finest hardware on the market (at vast expense) and you could be confident that you would be able to play the game at medium or high settings.

These days, minimum and recommended system requirements are pretty much useless to PC gamers and we have games consoles to thank for that fact. Games developers write games for all platforms, including Microsoft Xbox and Sony PlayStation as well as PC. Xbox 360 and PlayStation 3 are very similar and use hardware that dates from 2006 or 2007. In their day they were impressive, but Xbox One and PlayStation 4 are based on AMD hardware that properly belongs in a low-end and highly compact PC. By any rational standard these new consoles are weak-kneed and can barely play games at Full HD. In many cases these next-gen consoles actually play games at 720p HD.

Let's take a quick look at *Far Cry 4*:

Minimum system requirements
Intel Core i5-750 2.6GHz or AMD Phenom II X4 955 3.2GHz
NVIDIA GTX 460 or AMD Radeon HD 5850 1GB
4GB RAM
30GB storage

That Intel CPU dates from 2009 and costs £150 while the AMD CPU dates from 2011 and costs £80. The graphics hardware dates from early 2010 and costs about £150.

Recommended system requirements
Intel Core i5-2400S 2.5GHz or AMD FX-8350 4.0GHz
NVIDIA GTX 680 or AMD Radeon R9 290X 2GB
8GB RAM
30GB storage

Moving up to 'Recommended' requires an Intel CPU from 2011 that costs £170 while the AMD CPU dates from 2012 and costs £125. That level of graphics hardware costs about £250 and dates from the last year or two. This tells us a few things about the current state of PC hardware. The first is that Intel is a year or two ahead of AMD in terms of CPU technology, and the second is that AMD is much cheaper than Intel. If you want a certain amount of processing power, AMD is the cheaper way to go. On the other hand if you want the maximum in terms of performance and sophistication then Intel will deliver the goods, but it will cost you plenty of cash.

Graphics performance gives you a similar binary decision as

Far Cry 4 is a gorgeous looking game, providing you have the machine capable of running it.

you either choose AMD or NVIDIA. These companies leapfrog one another constantly and you will find that prices shift quickly to reflect the current state of play.

Those so-called next-generation gaming consoles use integrated AMD hardware that is very much aimed at the budget desktop PC. This hardware isn't suitable for gaming so the only way it can perform satisfactorily is by throttling the demands of the game. Typically the screen resolution is limited and the quality settings will also be pulled back from the maximum.

The main message is that a decent gaming PC will match or surpass the recommended system requirements and will allow you to play *Far Cry 4* at Full HD (1080p). The question is whether or not you can crank up the quality settings from medium to high or ultimate. And who says you only want to play at Full HD? What about dual or triple display or 4K? If you want to pump more pixels, you require more graphics and processing power, and that is when a gaming PC comes into its own.

Make no mistake about it, a gaming PC can offer you levels of performance that eclipse any games console, provided it is given the chance. We saw proof of this with *Watch Dogs*, which was developed and published by Ubisoft. To all intents and purposes *Watch Dogs* is *Grand Theft Auto V* with slightly fewer cars and rather more phone hacking. The original technical showcase and preview for *Watch Dogs* showed graphical details that were missing in the released game, presumably because the Xbox One and PlayStation 4 didn't have the ability to actually play the game with these features enabled. The surprise came when the PC version of the game was released as it also failed to live up to the promise of the original demo. Some modders worked on *Watch Dogs* and released a patch called TheWorse Mod that unlocks a number of features. We are familiar with texture packs that crunch through a game such as *Elder Scrolls Skyrim* and patch the graphics files so every object looks amazing. TheWorse Mod is much smaller than a texture pack and actually unlocks settings that were written into the game but which were then hidden away. The only logical conclusion is that Ubisoft knew full well the PC version of *Watch Dogs* would look superior to the console version and decided to level the playing field.

It makes sense to treat the game as part of your gaming PC. Ideally you simply play the game, but sometimes you need to go further and modify the game and give your gaming PC the chance to stretch its legs and show its pace.

So you've decided to build a new gaming PC from the ground up. Congratulations. Wise move. The starting point is to thrash out the specification of the hardware that you need, and that's not as easy as you might think. Let us sound a cautionary note: you might be tempted to upgrade your existing PC, but it usually makes better sense to build a new PC from scratch and then dispose of your old machine afterwards. If you intend to upgrade the motherboard, CPU and graphics card in your existing PC, you are basically keeping the case, power supply and DVD drive. That may sound like a useful financial saving, but there are good reasons to buy a complete set of new components. A case that is two or three years old will likely support 120mm cooling fans and a very old case will only have 80mm fans. New enthusiast hardware supports 140mm or 200mm fans. This provides more efficient cooling with low levels of noise as the larger fans can turn more slowly than their 120mm brothers.

Another change in cooling trends is a move away from air coolers towards all-in-one liquid cooling systems that require you to mount a fan and radiator inside your case in place of one or two of the existing fans. This is pretty much a straight swap, but you need to allow for the extra thickness of the hardware and you also require room for the water hoses, which is much more straightforward with a case that is designed for the job.

It is tempting to reuse a power supply that has done sterling duty for a few years. Let's face it, replacing a 650W power supply with another 650W PSU looks like a fine way to burn £90 of your hard-earned cash. The best way to think about your power supply is as an insurance policy. Of course you need the PSU to draw in 240V at one end and pump out 12V, 5V, 3.3V and plenty of amps at the other, but you also have to consider the amount of air and dust that has flowed through the power supply over the years. The problem is that when a power supply fails it can let go with an impressive bang and a certain amount of smoke, and this can send a spike through every component in the PC, destroying them all in the process.

By all means reuse your DVD drive, but for the small amount of £20 you might just as well start from scratch with a new model.

PART ② Research your build

It is pretty much impossible to pluck a price for a gaming PC from the air as there is such a huge variety of hardware. You can, however, say that £799 is a good starting point (for the tower, minus the monitor, mouse and keyboard), £999 is a psychological landmark, £1,299 gets you plenty and £1,999 is 'Ulp, how much?' If you go for the absolute maximum it is possible to spend £4,000, £6,000 or £8,000 on a gaming PC. To put that in context, some of us take a week's holiday in Cornwall or Spain while others head to the West Indies or safari in Kenya.

The ASRock X99 WS-E supports an Intel LGA2011 Extreme Edition CPU, although the price might make your eyes water.

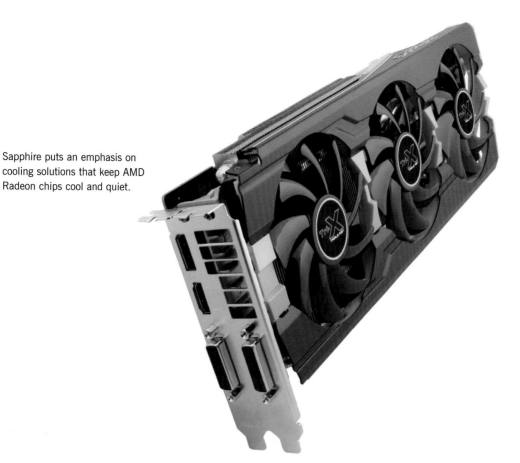

Sapphire puts an emphasis on cooling solutions that keep AMD Radeon chips cool and quiet.

The easiest way to start drafting the specification of your new gaming PC is to look at the website of one of the smaller PC builders. They will doubtless offer an array of PCs that you can customise using a series of drop-down menu options to select the components. This will rapidly give you a clear idea about the current state of gaming hardware and the cost of the components.

Let's break down a £1,250 PC build to get an idea of where the money goes. There is a range of prices for each component, but broadly speaking we can say:

£200–£300 on the graphics card
£150–£250 on the CPU
£100–£150 on the motherboard
£100 on a 250GB or 256GB SSD
£80 on the case
£80 on the power supply
£70–£100 on a 2TB or 3TB hard drive
£70 for 8GB of DDR3 memory
£70 on a liquid cooler or £40 for an air cooler for your CPU
£80 for a copy of Windows 8.1
£20 for a DVD drive
Total – circa £1,200

Those prices are guidelines to illustrate how you might break down the cost of a decent gaming PC, but in practice you can spend less on every component, or you can spend much more. The point here is to illustrate which components eat the bulk of the money, which is why the components are listed roughly in order of cost.

One thing is for certain: if you take a £799, £999, £1,299 or £1,999 PC from any of the manufacturers and break it down, you won't be able to build the same PC yourself for the same price. The fact you are paying retail prices means it will cost you more to build exactly the same PC and that's without allowing for the time you will invest or the convenience of having an assembled PC delivered to your door complete with a warranty.

Let's put it another way. If you see a PC listed on a manufacturer's website that matches your requirements in every respect, the wise move is to whip out your credit card and place an order since you'll be hard pushed to build it yourself any cheaper. That may sound like heresy in a book that aims to help you build your own PC, but of course the point is that you won't be building exactly the same PC as one that you find on sale. Instead of buying a PC that is almost what you want, you will instead build a PC that is exactly what you want.

The starting point is to decide how you wish to use your PC and then set yourself a guide price. It is worth taking a second look at the graphics part of the Recommended system requirements for

one of the biggest hits from last year, *Far Cry 4*. Either an NVIDIA GTX 680 or AMD Radeon R9 290X 2GB graphics card will do the trick, provided you are planning on using a single Full HD display. You might be able to push the resolution to 2,560×1,440, but if you intend to use multiple displays or 4K, you should think in terms of dual or even triple graphics cards. This is a major consideration as you can accommodate a single 300mm-length gaming graphics card in pretty much any PC case on the market. Dual graphics cards are also easy to accommodate although there is an obvious extra cost and you have to ensure that your power supply can deliver the necessary wattage. It is also worth checking that the power supply has the necessary PCI Express connectors for dual graphics cards.

Specifying triple graphics cards will have a dramatic impact on the system. You'll need a large case, full-size motherboard, hefty power supply and plenty of money as you will also need a high-end CPU to back up all that graphics hardware.

A fully loaded motherboard with three graphics cards is quite a sight to behold.

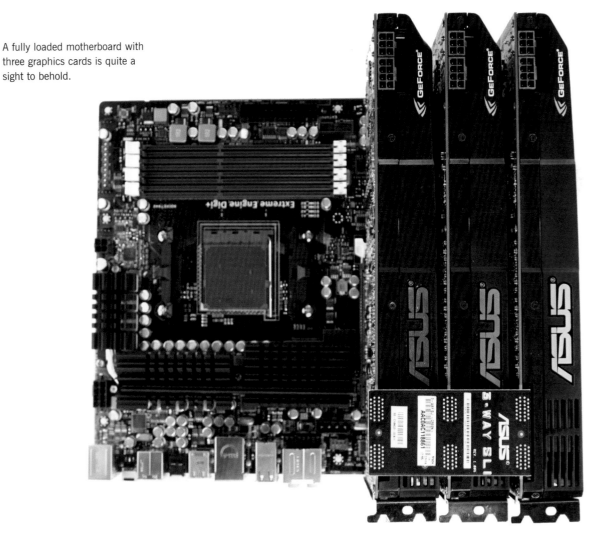

PART  Motherboards

This talk of graphics cards might seem like we are putting the cart before the horse. After all, everyone knows the CPU is the brain of your computer and so that, surely, is the correct place to start. Well no, not really. Start with an outline of your PC by thinking about how many graphics cards you want and that will help you nail down the form factor, which is a little like deciding whether your ideal accommodation would be an apartment, bungalow, house or mansion. The form factor has a huge impact on the finished gaming PC, and the main consideration boils down to the number of graphics cards, so let's look at your options.

Sapphire took a novel approach with the PURE Black 99FX by providing this motherboard with six PCI Express x16 slots.

There are something like 40 different form factors that have been sorted out by the computer industry to ensure that a given motherboard will fit inside a particular case and work with a certain power supply. Happily we can safely ignore obsolete, obscure and irrelevant form factors and concentrate on the four form factors that really matter.

The mainstream form factor is ATX (Advanced Technology Extended), which was created by Intel back in 1995. An ATX motherboard measures 305mm x 244mm and has six or seven expansion slots, which gives the manufacturer plenty of scope to offer a fair amount of variety. For example you might have two PCI Express x16 graphics slots, one PCI Express x4, two PCI Express x1 and two PCI. There is little or no expectation that you will populate all of those slots with expansion cards, and in many instances a dual slot graphics card will overhang the neighbouring slot and render that slot unavailable. You might install one or two graphics cards along with a sound card, but that will leave you with a fair amount of space that looks, at first glance, as though it has been wasted, but this is not necessarily so. Spacing out the cards allows cooling air to circulate and you will often find that routing cables is much easier if the graphics card is in *this* slot rather than *that* slot. An ATX motherboard will usually give you the option of moving hardware around, which includes using alternative SATA ports in a bid to make your life easy and also to tidy up the cosmetics of your PC build.

The worst reason for buying a large motherboard is the 'future upgrade path'. If you buy a motherboard with dual or triple graphics slots and install a single graphics card with the vague plan of installing a second graphics card in CrossFireX or SLI (CrossFireX was ATI's answer to NVIDIA's graphics-card linking technology, SLI) at a later date, then please think again. You might have sensible financial reasons for delaying the purchase of a second graphics card, but generally speaking this is a poor idea. For one thing you will need to buy a second graphics card that is near identical to the first and the easiest way to do that is to buy them simultaneously. The other thing is that CrossFireX and SLI can do strange things in certain games so you are best advised to buy one high end card rather than two mid-range cards.

In the past you could make the argument that most graphics cards only supported two or perhaps three display outputs so some set-ups with multiple monitors required dual graphics cards, purely to get the necessary connections. These days you can find graphics cards that support as many as six displays so you only need a second graphics card if you want serious gaming power or, perhaps, if you are building a computing-on-GPU system to mine Bitcoins.

The main alternative to ATX is Micro-ATX which measures 244mm x 244mm and has four expansion slots. Take an ATX board, cut out the middle section with three expansion slots and, bingo, you have a Micro-ATX board. Micro-ATX hardware is slightly cheaper than ATX as the design process is effectively free of charge and the construction requires slightly less in the way of materials and components. Choosing a Micro-ATX motherboard gives you the option of using a smaller case or you can stick with a regular ATX tower and take advantage of all the unused space inside.

Alternatively you can go to the other extreme and use an E-ATX or XL-ATX motherboard. The E stands for Extended ATX and measures 305mm x 330mm while XL-ATX (Extra Large)

It is possible to buy pre-built and ready to use motherboards that come with memory, a high-end CPU and often a dedicated processor.

measures approximately 330mm x 250mm. These monster motherboards are based on server technology and can support dual processors or up to four graphics cards. They are absolutely enormous and there are few options for super-large tower cases. You need to be quite certain that your bigger-than-ATX motherboard will fit inside your case.

Monster cases are big and bold, but there is nothing to stop you going in the opposite direction and choosing Mini-ITX. There are two distinct versions of this 170mm x 170mm form factor. A tiny system that uses a low-powered processor may well be housed in a case that is only slightly larger than the motherboard without any space for a graphics card or decent cooling. This is no good for the gamer.

The sort of Mini-ITX we might be interested in is a small motherboard with a single PCI Express expansion where the graphics card effectively hangs off the end of the board. The case needs only two expansion slots as it will only ever accommodate a single graphics card. The result should be a small and compact gaming PC that is highly portable and pretty much ideal for LAN parties yet it will pack in a full set of gaming features. Be warned: building a Mini-ITX PC is a bit like doing keyhole surgery and requires patience and a degree of dedication that isn't necessary when you work inside a larger case.

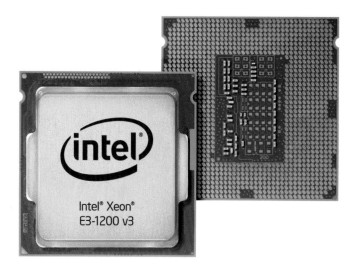

Intel's iSeries has been dominating the market for years now, but there are still differences in models and versions to look out for.

It is stating the obvious to point out that your case needs to be large enough to accept your chosen form factor of motherboard, but it is worth pointing out that you might choose to install a small motherboard in a larger case than appears strictly necessary. Certain Mini-ITX cases mount the motherboard horizontally in a case that is pretty much a cube so it is wider than a tower but quite a bit shorter. If you fancy building your own liquid cooling system, you may well find it makes sense to use a Micro-ATX motherboard in an ATX case, purely to give yourself some extra working room.

Anyone who wants three or four graphics cards should start with the expectation that they will use E-ATX and had better hope that their credit card matches their extra large expectations.

Slap bang in the mid-range we have the majority of PC builders who use an ATX motherboard in an ATX case with either one or two gaming graphics cards. This is an excellent place to be as your options are pretty much unlimited, but it also means you have plenty of scope to muck things up. Let's start to firm up the details and take a closer look at the specific hardware you'll be using to power your PC.

Some games are incredibly intensive on even the very best hardware, so consider the games you want to play before purchasing parts.

PART

Central Processing Unit (CPU)

Let's talk about processors. Specifically, let's talk about the CPU (Central Processing Unit), as opposed to the GPU (Graphics Processing Unit) or even the APU (Accelerated Processing Unit). The CPU is often referred to as the brain of your computer, but silicon can't really think for itself. In fact the CPU is just a very clever calculator that performs mathematical calculations measured in billions per second.

The problem with this analogy is that the CPU sends this torrent of numbers back and forth around the PC and in particular feeds a stream of data to your graphics card(s) where it is rendered as jaw-droppingly awesome pictures on your monitor(s). If you follow that way of thinking, the CPU is more like the heart of your PC than the brain, but no matter how you imagine it the CPU is hugely important.

The first step is to select the family of CPU that you want to use. This will enable you to settle on a particular CPU socket and a narrow selection of motherboard chipsets, and when you combine that with your chosen form factor you will be in a better position to choose the motherboard for your new PC.

There are only two mainstream contenders for the CPU market: AMD who has been playing the mouse to Intel's rather intimidating cat.

There are a number of features you need to consider when you compare one CPU with another, and we're going to look at those individually in turn. It is undoubtedly one of the most important – and most expensive – purchases you'll make for your gaming PC, but it does come with its own set of acronyms and jargon. Everything from the socket to the number of cores will likely confuse the layman. So rather than throw some examples into the mix and leave it at that we're first going to run down each of the elements you'll come across when buying a CPU.

Socket

What the term 'socket' denotes is simply the type of mechanical connection the processor chip has with the motherboard. Its purpose is to help you buy compatible parts and so long as you buy a motherboard that matches the socket type then, at least at a mechanical level, you'll have parts that fit together. Ordinarily you'll be looking at a socket 1150 for Intel CPUs and the AM3 (or AM3+) for AMD chips; so long as the sockets match up with your motherboard there are few other reasons to worry about this element.

To look at it you wouldn't notice much difference in an AMD setup when compared to an Intel one. Many of the parts will be similar.

Number of threads

In truth this is almost always correlative to the number of cores your CPU has. If there are four cores, it's highly likely there are four threads. Unless specifically told otherwise, processors will always complete the first task they're given before moving on to the next, and so the number of threads refers to the total number of applications able to be executed on the CPU at any one time. Four cores, four threads, four applications. However, some processors – typically Intel – offer a feature known as hyperthreading, whereby the operating system is told there are in fact twice the number of logical cores. While this doesn't actually increase the number of cores available, it allows for the processor to multi-task two applications per core and switch tasks far more easily. It's not a key aspect in CPU buying, but it's a nice added extra to look out for.

Core size

Measured in nanometers (nm) and relative to a single core on the CPU, the core size measurement is a factor you can largely ignore. If you're building a fairly typical computer – regardless of your budget – you'll likely encounter the numbers 14nm, 22nm or 32nm when it comes to a CPU's core size. If you're getting into the minutiae of hardware purchasing then it's worth knowing that a smaller core size will result in more efficient power consumption and computation speed, and in this regard Intel chips are currently ahead of the curve. But in truth the core size is a fairly insignificant factor to take into account when compared to some of the far more integral stats; don't be afraid to overlook core size when hunting for processors.

The CPU is one of the most delicate parts to install. This can intimidate a lot of people, but it's a very simple process.

Cores

If we consider a CPU to be a computer's brain, then the number of cores essentially denotes just how many brains it has. Back in the day a computer would have a single chip with which it could calculate computations, with the speed of that particular chip affecting how fast those processes would be. Nowadays CPUs can have multiple cores, giving them the ability to multi-task far more easily. This is especially important for videogames, where computations in physics systems and lighting rendering need to be performed while data needs to be streamed to the graphics card and hard drive – the more cores you have the more capable your machine is. At least in theory; you see, as common as multi-core processors are these days, games developers simply don't make complete use of their multi-processing capabilities, and so spending over the odds to increase the number and speed of those cores is going to end up as wasted money. If you find you're likely to take part in processor-intensive activities, however, such as 3D design or video editing and rendering, then you may want to consider aiming for more cores rather than more speed. Quad core is the most common you'll come across, though cheaper CPUs can come with dual cores while six and eight cores are becoming increasingly more common – even if their costs are a little prohibitive at the moment. AMD has even released behemoth CPUs with 12 and 16 cores, but that's a little on the excessive side – especially considering the limitations that games often have with regards to the number of CPU cores they use. Ultimately it comes down to a choice: if you're going to be regularly putting strain on your computer with computation-heavy processes and regularly multitasking in these situations then you'll want to get yourself a CPU with a larger number of cores. If gaming is all you're aiming for, then a quad-core chip will more than satisfy your needs.

Core name

This is little more than the terminology given by the manufacturer – basically Intel or AMD – for the particular make and model of the cores installed on the processor. These are changing all the time, and even within particular families of chips the particular core model is often upgraded, changed or improved. Take, for example, Intel's latest iSeries of processors, which began life named Sandy Bridge, became Ivy Bridge and now we're onto Haswell and Broadwell. The particular name of a model will forever be changing, and that's not something we can really help with; you can usually spot the most up-to-date and recent chipset via the price (newer models will cost more), but don't be afraid to search for the information if you're at a loss. The name itself is irrelevant, but it's an easy way to spot-check just how new the CPU you're buying is, providing you research the most recent chipset of the series.

Clock/Turbo speed

Most CPUs will come with two measurements with regards to their speed: 'Clock' and 'Turbo'. The term clock is something you'll come across a lot when tinkering with your PC, and essentially it refers to a measurement of speed when compared to the computer's internal, mechanical clock – by which everything on the system is timed. A CPU's Clock speed, then, is its base speed, and is used to detail the speed at which the processor will run when it is not under load. This is an important stat, for sure, since the processor should never drop below this speed, but since you'll be gaming on this PC – and therefore tasking your processor – you should also take note of the Turbo speed. This is how fast the processor can run when it is under load – or, in other words, being used to compute intensive tasks like gaming – and will essentially denote its maximum capacity. This is actually one of the most important elements to look out for on your hardware purchasing travels, and should be a factor you take seriously when buying parts.

FSB/QPI/DMI/HT Speed

Are these acronyms really all that important? Well, yes and no. In all likelihood only one of them will be present on your processor, and each acronym refers to the type of 'bus' used in the processor. A computer's 'bus' – as you might expect – is the vehicle through which data is transferred from the CPU to the rest of the hardware. The speed of this part, then, will affect the speed with which other elements – such as your graphics card or memory – can receive and send back data to the central brain of your computer. As with a bus that you might travel on, the faster it travels the quicker it arrives at its destination. The acronyms, however, aren't all that important in and of themselves. FSB is perhaps the most common, albeit increasingly outdated, while newer ones – such as DMI – can transfer up to 20 Gigatransfers a second (GT/s). You may also find this measured in MHz – or megahertz – and there is a distinction. MHz is a bus's speed, while GT/s is the number of transfers it can make. While speed

Overclocking the CPU is the most common method of enhancing the potential technical limit of your PC, but you'll need an upgraded cooling system to survive the increased temperatures.

is important when it comes to your computer's bus, modern architecture demands that the number of transfers capable of being made is equally important. In that regard a bus's width is often more important than its speed; to use the transportation analogy again, if a bus can carry twice as many people, at max capacity it is able to transport more passengers than a smaller bus. Thankfully you don't really need to worry too much about the methodology of it all; just understand that the higher this number is – however it is measured – the better for your system's overall performance.

Max memory size and speed

As sad as it is to say, your system memory – or RAM – is always finding itself limited in some way, whether that's through your operating system's restrictions or even the available slots in the motherboard. Even the processor you buy will limit the maximum memory you can have in your computer, in many cases limiting it to 32GB of RAM. While this doesn't mean you can't install more than that into the motherboard itself, sadly the processor simply won't 'see' that much memory there, and you'll need to install a second processor to enable a larger stack of memory. Take note of this – especially the memory speed – since this will ultimately guide the absolute limit you can aim for when buying RAM.

Intel might be a fair bit more expensive, but the efficiency that their CPUs provide are – currently – unmatched in the market.

Voltage, wattage and temperature

The last thing you're going to want to look out for is the power consumption of your CPU, though in truth it's rare that this will ever impact (or even differ between) your purchasing decisions. As with all parts in your machine, the power that your CPU uses correlates to the temperature that it will run at – the more power, the higher the temperature. This is the single most important aspect of careful maintenance, because when your parts run too hot they are at a risk of becoming damaged. You may not get all of the information regarding these attributes, or you may only get its power consumption rather than the temperature (or vice versa), so try to use comparable parts as a reference point. It's most important to take note of the CPU's TDP (Thermal Design Power), which is the point at which the CPU is too hot to function. While this likely won't ever be a problem under ordinary circumstances, if it does overheat it will likely throttle the performance of the processor, making your machine run incredibly slowly or, in worst-case scenarios, shut off the CPU altogether. If you overclock your machine (which we'll talk about later), or find you are regularly stressing your CPU beyond its TDP, then you'll need to take precautions to ensure the problem is resolved – either by adding more cooling systems to your PC, reducing any overclocking you have done, or even replacing the thermal paste of the CPU.

Intel or AMD?

This is a common question when it comes to CPUs, but in truth the answer is rather easy to provide. While there are a handful of other CPU designers on the market, most are aimed at specialised markets – mobile, low-power consumption and the like – rather than more general-purpose hardware. When it comes to PC gaming, the processor industry really is a two-horse race, and the current leader has been ahead in the race for years.

Intel's control of the CPU market – as it stands – is unwavering. Its most recent iSeries range – i3, i5 and i7 – have proven very popular, a fine balance between efficiency and power and a stability that all hardware purchasers hope for. It maintains its Pentium and Celeron range for low-budget alternatives – not something we really need to concern ourselves with – as well as its Xeon range, which offers many more cores per CPU than the typical quad core. This range is more in line with large-scale servers for businesses and – again – not really something we need to consider. As such it's the iSeries that you'll want to look into for a gaming PC, and though the cost is slightly increased over an AMD equivalent it's worth drawing attention to the company's reputation – there's no smoke without fire, as they say, and Intel is well known for producing high-quality processors that are well worth their cost.

AMD, on the other hand, has been struggling for years under the dominance of Intel. The difference is that Intel also manufactures its CPUs, so it is able to more easily implement new methods of production as it innovates on its designs. AMD's answer to this is to provide its CPUs at a cheaper price, hoping to clean up the budget market. As with Intel it manages lines for low-end and server-focused CPUs, with its current FX range being the one for gamers. The difference here – besides price – is AMD's emphasis on extra cores, with a eight-core processor coming out at around the same price as a quad-core Intel equivalent. As discussed earlier, more cores doesn't necessarily mean better gaming so this might not be a worthwhile option – however, if you're looking to shave some of the costs off your system then switching from Intel to AMD will give you that opportunity.

AMD certainly plays second fiddle in this two-horse race, but its cheaper CPUs and preference for a high number of cores make it a strong competitor.

PART  # System memory

System memory or RAM is a major part of your PC build and the cost can be significant with 32GB kits of DDR4 costing around £400. That's a lot of money but DDR4 is new technology and currently limited to a tiny handful of people, including those who use the Intel Extreme Edition LGA2011, so most of us can breathe a sigh of relief and focus on DDR3.

There are three factors to consider: the number of modules, the capacity of the modules and the clock speed of the memory. There are hundreds of combinations of makes and models, but perhaps the starting point should be the heat spreaders. That may sound like a cosmetic point, but you need to be sure the memory will fit in your motherboard and won't interfere with a high-end air cooler. On the other hand, if you are using liquid cooling then you can be confident the heat spreaders won't pose a problem.

How much memory do you need? Assuming you are using 64-bit Windows you can literally run as much memory as you can afford (32-bit software is limited to 4GB) although you are unlikely to gain much benefit from installing more than 8GB. There is no harm in spending the extra cash on 16GB but 32GB is a completely frivolous luxury. Assuming you have a dual-channel

HyperX Beast DDR3 memory is big, tall and visually striking, and also as fast as heck.

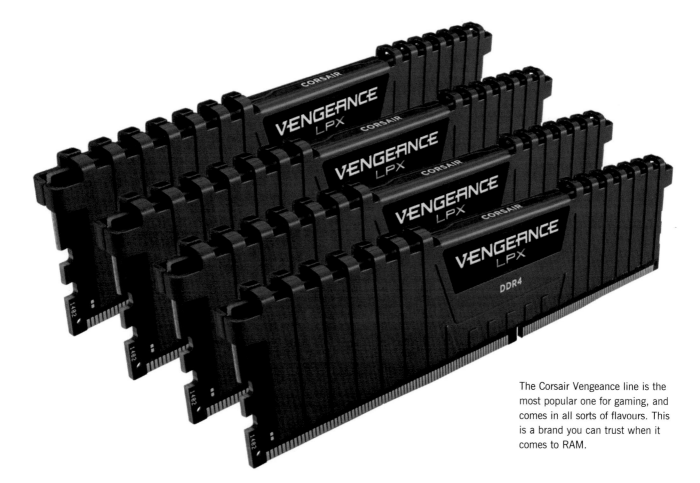

The Corsair Vengeance line is the most popular one for gaming, and comes in all sorts of flavours. This is a brand you can trust when it comes to RAM.

memory controller you should stick to two modules of memory. In theory you can install four modules, but this can cause problems with incompatibility and can also slow performance.

When you install your shiny new DDR3 and enable AMP or XMP in the BIOS to increase the speed from the default 1,333MHz or 1,600MHz to the rated speed of 1,866MHz, 2,133MHz or 2,400MHz you may feel a warm glow when you think about the extra bandwidth you have unlocked. In fact this DDR3 bandwidth is almost entirely an illusion so by all means buy memory that comes with a solid guarantee of reliability and, yes, go for a groovy heat spreader that is colour co-ordinated to your new PC, but don't get too stressed about the clock speed.

But, perhaps more than any piece of hardware, RAM can come with numerous acronyms – all of which won't make much sense. We'll run down some of the more important ones, and what you need to look for:

Memory type

DIMM, DRAM, DDR, SDRAM; there are all sorts of types of memory and it can get a little overwhelming. Some types even have their own specialised acronyms for specific models – and frankly it's all a little much. DDR is the most common and easily the most reliable and compatible type to fit into a gaming PC. Though, in truth, DDR itself has since evolved into DDR2, DDR3 and the most recent model DDR4. Think of this as new iPhones being released every year; there's always going to be a newer, faster model; what's important is picking the right one for you.

Mercifully you won't find too much out of the ordinary when it comes to shopping for memory since, as we say, DDR is the most common by far. If budget isn't a problem then it's certainly worth picking up a set of DDR4 memory sticks, but so long as you get a high-end DDR3 set you won't notice much difference – and your wallet will thank you too.

Memory size

This is perhaps the most significant number to look out for when buying RAM, if only because it directly correlates to the amount of data the RAM will handle. Remember that most processors will be limited to 32GB of RAM – so don't worry too much about jamming 64GB in there – but in truth 32GB is easily more than enough. If you're looking to save money on your budget then 8GB will more than suffice, but for a little extra cost you'll likely be able to get 16GB instead. There are plenty of options available, so make sure you shop around to find out what is best for you. Whatever you do, don't confuse this with your RAM's speed – memory size is simply the amount of data your RAM can handle at any one time, the higher that number the more it can do before the system begins to slow down.

Memory channel

It's imperative that you take note of the memory channel, and make sure it matches up with that of your motherboard. The channel simply refers to the optimal setup for the number of individual memory sticks, and in most cases memory kits are sold as complete channel packages – often denoted by the description of the RAM itself, for example 2X8GB meaning there are two sticks of RAM in the kit. Dual channel is the most common and will likely be the one you need to pick for your motherboard, but kits can come in triple- and quad-channel too. It's worth noting that you can remove individual memory sticks from a kit and still have it function well, but for the added expense it's better to make sure you buy a channel that corresponds with your motherboard's capabilities. Additionally, while you can install quad-channel kits into a dual-channel motherboard (where space allows), it's important to know that this can lead to issues that can reduce functionality. Due to the way the motherboard may detect the memory, it may not detect the additional memory at all; its timings may be totally off (affecting system stability) and could even reduce the 'visible' memory total to a single memory unit. To avoid any problems, it's better to buy matching memory channels.

Speed and latency

The two biggest elements to affect how fast your memory works is speed (otherwise known as frequency) and its latency. The frequency – measured in MHz and often in denominations 1,333MHz, 1,600MHz and 2,400MHz – is a measurement of the RAM's bandwidth, and affects how much data can be moved to and from it at a time. Latency, instead, affects how quickly data can be transferred from the RAM and this can be a very confusing statistic to look up. Often seen as CAS Latency (seen as a set of numbers, such as 9-9-9-24) the key here is to look for lower numbers, rather than higher – the opposite of many of the parts you'll be buying. This is the 'timing' of the RAM – how long between actions; the lower the time between actions, the faster that RAM will work – and you'll likely spend a bit more for a CAS Latency beginning with 9 (the first number, while not the only important one, is the one to look out for).

DDR4 is very new technology and currently restricted to certain CPU and motherboard systems. If you want the absolute best, make sure you get parts that are compatible.

Buying RAM new almost always comes in packages, making it an easy way to detect what channel the memory will optimally run in.

However, usually when one of these figures improves it is at the expense of the other; your RAM may think faster, but as a result it will be able to handle less data. In truth the extra speed doesn't actually offer much in the way of performance gains, which means it's about finding that balance. If DDR3 is the RAM you're going for then a CAS Latency of 9 or 10 with a frequency or speed of 1600–1800 will be the best option.

XMP and AMP

You'll never get a stick of RAM capable of XMP and AMP – because they're both exactly the same, only AMP is the AMD version of the otherwise more common XMP. All memory as it is bought comes with its 'safe' setting, a profile that is a little below the true potential of the RAM that adjusts the timings (latency) and frequency to settings lower than it is actually capable of. This is to ensure there are few problems – since hardware can be installed on a whole range of machines, and compatibility is a manufacturer's prime concern. Nowadays many memory kits come with XM or AM profiles, in-built settings that can be manually activated to get the optimal performance out of your RAM without having to overclock it or adjust settings yourself. If this feature is present, don't be afraid to use it.

High-end memory often comes in a variety of colours; if you're planning on having a windowed case for your PC then don't be afraid to pick a colour that matches your build.

PART

Graphics cards

So far we have covered form factor, motherboards, processors and memory, yet graphics have barely merited a mention. When you consider that an NVIDIA GeForce GTX 980 sells for the thick end of £500 it is quite easy to spend £1,000 for an SLI set-up, so graphics are a huge consideration.

Happily, unless you are deeply involved in the finer points of overclocking, we don't need to know a huge amount about the technology behind graphics cards. There are only two companies in the gaming graphics chip market, AMD (which bought ATI) and NVIDIA, who consistently leapfrog each other as they develop new graphics chips and come up with clever ideas to make gameplay better. The wonderful thing for gamers is that AMD and NVIDIA GPUs have to work with a number of important technologies and this means that modern graphics cards are interchangeable in a gaming PC, provided we install the correct driver software to allow the card to work properly.

Microsoft Windows includes a framework called DirectX, which allows graphics cards, games, drivers and Windows to all work nicely together. In the past each new version of DirectX introduced significant features such as Transform and Lighting, Vertex Shaders, Pixels Shaders and High Dynamic Range

NVIDIA ruled the roost with the GTX 980. While it is expensive the results are stunning.

For the cost, the GTX Titan is more of a luxury option. If budget is no concern, however, this is a beast of a card that will take anything you throw at it.

Lighting, but in recent times things have settled down. Microsoft introduced DirectX 11 with Windows 7 and updated to DX11.1 with Windows SP1 and will introduce DirectX 12 with Windows 10. As yet we don't know what new features will come with DX12, but we do know that current hardware will work with Windows 10, although they are unlikely to support all of the features of the new framework.

The really good news is that both AMD and NVIDIA support PCI Express 3.0 and the same 6-pin and 8-pin power connectors that you find on any decent power supply. Naturally they use DVI, HDMI and DisplayPort connections to hook up to your display(s). This means we are able to treat these competing graphics cards as a simple lump of graphics power, provided we never attempt to combine an AMD card with an NVIDIA card in the same PC.

At present NVIDIA's technology trumps AMD's for efficiency and low power draw while delivering high performance, and the nature of the graphics market means that AMD has been forced to drop their prices to make up for their technological deficit.

AMD and NVIDIA sell GPUs and reference cards to a whole host of partners (Asus, EVGA, Gigabyte, KFA2, MSI, Palit, Powercolor, Sapphire and Zotac among others). Many graphics cards use a reference design while others distinguish themselves with an aftermarket cooler in a bid to reduce noise and heat.

Most of us are perfectly happy to buy a graphics card with 2GB of GDDR5 memory although very high-resolution screens may benefit from 4GB, 6GB or even 8GB of memory. We'll ignore dual-GPU models such as Radeon R9 295 X2 as they are thin on the ground, awfully expensive and not much different to a pair of graphics cards in CrossFireX or SLI. Once you settle on a particular GPU you can then choose whether or not to buy a factory overclocked model.

Here's a quick and dirty guide to the current crop of graphics cards:

£450–£550 GeForce GTX 980
£299 GeForce GTX 970
£230–£299 Radeon R9 290
£199 Radeon R9 285
£175 GeForce GTX 960
£150 Radeon R9 280
£125–£150 Radeon R9 270

NVIDIA often redesign existing models and release them as 'Ti' versions, with better efficiency, power consumption or even overall graphical capabilities.

This throws up a few pointers as the GTX 970 looks like better value than the GTX 980, and anyone on a budget should choose the GTX 960. Both the Radeon R9 285 and R9 290 do a fine job, but they demand more power than the GeForce GTX 9xx so they need to be cheap to get your attention. If you dip down as far as Radeon R9 280 or 270 then it is questionable whether you truly have a gaming PC, rather than a PC that can play games.

As with all technological parts there are a number of different jargon terms to understand if you hope to make the right purchase. Sticking with some of the previous examples will see you safe, but to truly make your PC your own – and to keep it within your own budget – it's better to know what to look for:

Manufacturer

While there are only really two designers of GPUs – AMD and NVIDIA – there are a number of manufacturers, and while that might be confusing for the first-time buyer it's actually much better for consumers since it keeps prices down and invigorates competition. As with all such things, however, some manufacturers are better than others, and that's an always-changing, dynamic system. The likes of Asus, MSI, EVGA and Gigabyte are all well-reputed for their quality products with a competitive price – you won't need to pay over the odds to get a decent GPU from one of these manufacturers. Picking a manufacturer is not an easy task, but nor is it really one we can help with – just check out some reviews of different GPUs and if they are primarily positive and talk about the graphics card's reliability and build quality then you should know it's from a trustworthy manufacturer. Just be vigilant and you should have few problems, since the better products have a tendency to rise to the top anyway.

Memory

The beauty of buying a graphics card is that, by and large, look for a large memory number from a trusted manufacturer and in all likelihood you'll have a card worth buying. That's not a hard-and-fast rule, of course, but it highlights the significance of your memory. The more memory your card has the more it'll cost – since it is capable of creating even better visuals as a result. As such your budget will largely determine what size memory you should go for. At 2GB you'll likely have no problems running most games – even some of the high-end ones – but it won't futureproof you by any stretch. NVIDIA is already dominating the market with its recent 9xx series, low-power but incredibly efficient 4GB cards that you should really consider. Of course you can go further, too, with 6GB and even 8GB cards available on the market – though currently those are very much high-end, luxury items. It's better to shop around within your budget rather than devote yourself to a particular number of memory, but more is very much better when it comes to a smooth gaming experience.

Cores

This will likely confuse newcomers since many websites advertise the number of cores as a primary feature of GPUs rather than, as we say, the size of the memory. Well there is some significance to it, and ultimately the number of cores tells you how speedy a particular GPU is. It's not a strict comparison that needs making since some cards can use fewer cores more efficiently or to compute more complex tasks, but it's a good value to compare all the same. The higher the number of cores the quicker that card will be able to run; of course it's not quite as simple as that, but these days the number of cores is often quite comparable – so don't worry yourself too much about this aspect. As with your card's memory, instead shop within your budget rather than stressing too much about the number of cores.

Core/Boost Clock

Tying into the total number of cores is the individual core speed, and a way in which some cards with the same number of cores (or even less) can be more capable than others. Imagine cores as tiny engines for your graphics card: the Core Clock speed – measured in MHz – denotes just how fast that engine can work. That means a higher figure here will denote a card whose cores can work quicker than competitors, so it's a good – albeit not imperative – measurement to consider. Boost Clock, however, is the speed that the GPU is capable of; as with all PC hardware, GPUs are sold at an underperforming rate to keep it safe for your system and for the card's longevity. While you won't need to increase that clock speed initially, it's good to take note of the potential of it all the same – it'll help you understand its potential should you want to overclock it in the future.

More fans on a card ultimately means two things: it won't be as affected by heat, and it will more likely make noise when under load.

Cooling

Every GPU will come with its own on-board fan, a necessary method to keep your card cool while it's busy creating all those lovely on-screen graphics. It will be taking the brunt of the processing for 3D gaming, so keeping it cool is imperative. Manufacturer's methods and preferences for cooling changes from card to card, and in truth great strides have been made in power consumption over the last few years so you may not need to worry too much about cooling. With that said, it's always worth spending just a little bit extra to get a card that comes with at least two on-board fans – it's just a little extra security, on top of your own cooling systems, to ensure your GPU is treated well. You can get cards with three fans, too, but these end up being smaller and have to work harder (and louder) as a result; and the benefits in cooling they provide isn't all that noticeable.

Power supply

Since the GPU in your PC is going to be the part that is eating up well over half of your machine's power – at least under load –

you should be aware of the amount of juice you're going to need to power it. This will directly affect what power supply unit you'll need to buy, after all. Luckily the details on these cards often have both its demand and a suggested supply unit. The demand will depend entirely on the cards you're looking at and how powerful they are, but you'll be looking at the low end of 150W up to and even over 300W – though GPUs are becoming much more efficient (and therefore less power hungry). You'll actually want a power demand that is lower, since that means the card will run cooler and quieter as a result – but remember demand is correlative to its power as a GPU, so you won't get a high performance card with too low a consumption.

SLI/CrossFire

Most dedicated gaming graphics cards offer SLI or CrossFire functionality these days, so you won't need to worry about it all that much. They're both terms for the ability to run two or more GPUs alongside one another, effectively doubling your potential graphical output (as well as the cost). It's very much a high-end method and if you want the absolutely most powerful machine then this is an option you'll want to consider – but as a result you'll need to take into account your power supply, case size, motherboard, cooling systems and even a processor capable of running it without a bottleneck. Of course you can add an additional card in SLI/ CrossFire later on, but if you're going to do it we'd recommend buying two of the same cards simultaneously to avoid any problems – technology changes all the time, and there's no guarantee you'll find a card matching yours when the time comes.

The GTX9xx series is incredibly power efficient and so shouldn't overheat too much by itself, but it's still always better to spend a little bit more for dual fans.

Though the connections the card is capable of might seem insignificant, it's important to know for when it comes to buying a monitor and connection cables.

Connectivity and dimensions

Perhaps this is only a small factor in the grand scope of your GPU, but it's still important all the same. Dimensions, first and foremost, are integral since you'll want to be sure your new card actually fits. This is both its physical size – so as to fit within your case – as well as the number of slots it'll take up on your motherboard. Usually these slots will be PCI Express (or PCIe) and for a typical gaming PC GPU it'll likely take up two slots. In most situations you'll have no problems in this regard since there's a fair degree of standardisation to sizes these days – but it's worth checking to be certain all the same. Connectivity, too, is important since it tells you through what means your GPU will display images onto your monitor. This is good to know since one affects the purchase of the other, and you'll want to know you can utilise that beast of a GPU to the very best by connecting through the best possible video cable.

Tips for picking the right GPU

We can probably guess just how you feel at this point. Graphics cards are perhaps the most important part of any gaming PC, and with so many options available it can seem a little overwhelming – even when armed with the necessary info to make a good decision. For newcomers to PC building there's always going to be a paranoid sensation that the GPU you've bought is, in some small way, inferior to another you had eyed. It's safe to ignore that sensation; that's not necessarily doubt that is talking but instead the confusion of wariness and apprehension over the cost – so long as you've come to a decision that is within your budget, provides for your gaming needs and perhaps even offers a little room for future-proofing then you should be satisfied.

But we also know that confident words of assurance won't help, so if you really need assistance prior to making that costly purchase then consider user reviews. Many websites include a rating system, while others even feature written reviews from customers, and while it's not a clear cut reason to trust in a purchase it will likely ease some concerns (or answer them, even) in seeing other customers explain their experiences with the graphics card. If you select a handful of potential purchases then you can use the general consensus of opinion to make your ultimate decision. It helps to look at the number of reviews available, too; if one card has a much higher number of reviews placed than another, you can safely assume that the former is much more popular – and it being popular means it's also probably the better product.

Alternatively you can use benchmarks. Numerous tech websites use benchmarks to better compare the capabilities of different GPUs, whether that's bespoke systems to rate and compare numerous different cards or benchmark images included as part of their professional reviews. Since so many different factors can alter the performance of a card, using these benchmarks can be a great way to find out which of your selected GPUs will provide the better gaming experience.

PART ②

Power supply units (PSU), storage and cases

It is easy to think of the PSU as a simple box that takes in mains voltage at one end and spits out 12V, 5V and 3.3V at the other end along with a colossal level of amperage. You pay £50 for a basic PSU and as much as £200 for a high-end 1,200W modular unit, which sounds terribly expensive. In fact, a quality PSU is the cheapest insurance you will ever buy.

For one thing a decent PSU is loaded with a variety of protection circuits that guard against spikes in voltage and current and can handle high temperatures and other nastiness. Load a quality PSU to its rated limit and it will continue to power your CPU and graphics cards without any fuss, drama, heat or noise. By contrast a poor quality PSU will start to lose efficiency as it approaches its rated limit and will get hot, which may lead to increased fan noise. That's all well and good when the PSU is new, but after a few years of hard work and an awful lot of airflow and dust you'll want the reassurance that your PSU will continue to deliver good service.

Choosing a suitable PSU is more difficult than you might expect as some companies manufacture their own hardware while others carry out the design and subcontract to Chinese manufacturers. Other brands simply take an existing model and add their own logo. It is common to find one brand selling a large range of PSUs where the budget models are sourced from one manufacturer while premium models are sourced from another.

Be aware of cheaper power supply units; though you'll be saving money in the short term it could cost you in the long term.

Modular PSUs will allow for much more freedom in connections, as well as a much tidier end result after putting your PC together.

When you buy a PSU you obviously need to ensure the power rating is sufficient to deliver the juice for your hardware. Unless you run dual or triple graphics cards you may be surprised to find that a 550W or 650W unit is more than enough for your needs. It is critical that you check the details of any PSU to make sure it has the connections you need, for example whether you need two 6-pin and two 8-pin PCI Express connectors. It is worth double-checking that the cables will reach across your motherboard to the connection points. Some combinations of case and motherboard require cables that are longer than the standard 60cm, while some budget PSUs have cables that are only 50cm long.

The 80 Plus efficiency rating is a good guide to the quality of the PSU – Bronze is adequate, Silver is good and Gold is excellent. Platinum and Titanium are very high-end and cost more, but if you can afford higher quality then it makes a lot of sense. This isn't just a question of saving money on wasted electricity. If your Bronze 650W PSU is running at 50% load you can expect it to be 85% efficient, which suggests 50W is being converted into heat. By contrast a Gold PSU should be 92% efficient, which implies 26W of wasted power, and a considerably lower amount of heat being pumped into the guts of your PSU and then out into the airstream.

Most premium PSUs are modular, which means you can detach the cables you don't need to avoid excess clutter. This is very handy when you need, for example, plenty of SATA connections but no Molex 4-pin connections. The main reason for using a modular PSU is to avoid having unused PCI Express cables festooned around the innards of your case as they look a complete mess and can affect airflow for your cooling.

Storage

Any gaming PC should use a Solid State Drive (SSD) rather than a Hard Disk Drive (HDD) as the difference in performance is considerable. An SSD operates at around 300–500MBps while a fast hard drive is unlikely to top 200MBps. Add in the tiny 2.5-inch form factor of an SSD compared to a 3.5-inch HDD and the fact that SSD is silent and it makes the argument pretty much a no-brainer. In fact HDD still has the edge on capacity as you can buy a 1TB SSD for £350–£500 while desktop HDD technology goes all the way to 6TB for less than £200. There is another version of SSD that uses a form factor called M.2, looks like a laptop Wi-Fi card and is installed in a suitable slot directly on your motherboard.

If you want performance then SSD is the only sensible option, but of course you could choose to install a 256GB SSD for £100 or a 500GB drive for £200 and then add a few terabytes of hard drive for bulk storage. You can buy a 2TB or 3TB HDD for £100–£130.

At the time of writing, the Samsung 850 EVO was the number one best-selling solid state storage solution on the market.

Basic hard drives can come with multiple terabytes of space, so much potential storage you likely won't need to upgrade for a long while.

It may surprise you, but the case is perhaps the most important part of your hardware purchasing. It affects your purchasing options for practically every other part.

It's difficult to find that balance between aesthetics and functionality with a case, but it can be done.

Although SSD drives look the same from the outside there are plenty of differences inside the casing. Controller chips, firmware and memory technology vary from one drive to another and luckily you don't need to worry too much about the details for a gaming PC. SLC (Single-Level Cell) memory technology is better than MLC (Multi-Level Cell) while TLC (Triple-Level Cell) is used for USB drives and media devices.

The easiest rule of thumb is to check the warranty to explain the difference between one drive and another. For example the Samsung 850 EVO uses 3-bit MLC memory and has a 5-year warranty, while the Samsung 850 Pro uses 2-bit MLC and has a 10-year warranty. The 250GB version of 850 EVO costs £110 while the 256GB 850 Pro costs £150, which pretty much tells you all you need to know about cost versus quality.

If you are looking to save money then you can forgo an SSD in place of a traditional HDD, and the size of it will depend on your budget and how much you anticipate installing. Modern games can easily take up 20GB or more, so while a 1TB drive might be sufficient it'll eventually require you to juggle a bit more than you might like. Opting for 2TB will see you safe for the foreseeable future.

There isn't really much more to buying PC storage than that, though considering factors like RPM and data transfer speed will ensure you get a drive that can at least transfer data quicker. It's secondary to finding a good drive, however, so read reviews to make sure you're getting something reliable first and foremost.

Cases

The final component to round out your PC build is the case. In some senses the case is little more than a smart box that holds your hardware. However if the CPU is the heart of your PC and the graphics card the muscles that do the heavy lifting then the case is the skin and skeleton. In the first instance your case needs to be large enough to accommodate your chosen motherboard and graphics card(s). The case supports all of your hardware and also presents a cosmetic face to the world, which makes a personal statement about your gaming PC.

It makes a big difference whether you want a heavily perforated case with loads of cooling fans or you want to install an AIO liquid cooler for the CPU and perhaps another AIO for your graphics card.

Fundamental questions about your new PC include the number of 2.5-inch and 3.5-inch drive bays that you require. You might decide that you don't want an optical drive, and that decision cleans up the front panel of your PC and also frees up a load of space inside.

A tidy PC build means you need a decent amount of space behind the motherboard tray, and if you do a good job, you could show the results to the world with a windowed side panel. Other neat touches in certain cases include a power supply cover that keeps all those messy cables out of sight.

While your case won't affect the performance of your gaming PC, it has a huge impact on the ease of the build, as well as

The Akasa Venom Toxic is an example of a full tower case that can accommodate an EATX motherboard.

the cooling and noise levels, and that makes it well worth some careful consideration.

Cooling

You can cool your gaming PC very effectively with an air cooler, but, honestly, you would do much better with an All-in-One (AIO) liquid cooler. Where an air cooler heats up the air in the middle of your case an AIO transfers the heat to the radiator at the back, top, front or bottom of your case and then it is only a short distance to the outside air. AIO coolers use 120mm or 150mm fans and radiators are sized at 120mm, 240mm, 360mm, 140mm and 280mm, which gives you plenty of options. Prices start below £50 and go up to £125 or thereabouts. It is certainly possible to spend as little as £25 on a reasonable air cooler, but a performance model will cost £50–75 so liquid coolers are actually highly competitive. There are plenty of brands in the AIO market such as Antec, Cooler Master, Corsair, NZXT and Thermaltake although the hardware is made by Asetek or CoolIT so these systems have a fair amount in common. The differences come down to the length of the coolant hoses and differences in USB monitoring software. All of these coolers do a fine job and you are unlikely to hit a problem, whichever system you choose.

Self-contained water cooling systems like this one from Corsair are very effective and quiet in operation.

PART **3** # Build a gaming PC

We need a smooth 60 frames per second from today's hottest games, but that's possible without breaking the bank...

To most people £1,500 is a lot of money, but it's easy enough to spend this much when it comes to building a truly high-end gaming PC – it's perfectly possible to blow that entire budget on a graphics card and processor alone. Chapter 1's buying advice taught us that more money doesn't equal more performance, however, and there's a limit to the sensible performance return on monetary investment. The more you spend, the lower the realistic return.

• NZXT Source 340 mid-tower case	**£60**
• Gigabyte X99 Gaming 5 motherboard	**£200**
• Intel Haswell-E 5820K 3.30GHz CPU	**£310**
• Corsair H100i water cooler	**£90**
• MSI GeForce GTX 970 4GB graphics card	**£300**
• Crucial PC4-17000 CL16 16GB DDR4 RAM	**£130**
• Samsung 840 EVO 2.5in 250GB SSD	**£110**
• Seagate 2TB SSHD 3.5in Hard Drive	**£90**
• Corsair CX750 PSU	**£70**
TOTAL COST	**£1,360**

We've picked our components to maximise bang for buck from our £1,500 budget.

That gets us a lot of quality gaming performance and enough change from £1,500 to buy a decent gaming monitor too. The biggest single investment in this system is the Haswell-E Intel processor standing at just under a quarter of the entire budget. We also spent a relatively high portion of the budget on a very versatile (and overclocking friendly) motherboard. The X99 chipset is fast and connectivity is off the scale.

The NVIDIA GeForce 970 may have got a rough ride from the press when it was released (there were several inaccuracies surrounding its specifications upon its initial launch), but it still does exactly what it set out to do by offering blazing fast frame rates for today's hottest games at a realistic price point. We could have thrown 150% more money at our graphics card, and only seen a return of 20%. In terms of raw frames per second, we're talking about practically imperceptible improvements.

Finally, we went to town on storage. As you should already know, solid-state hard drives represent one of the biggest performance improvements in recent years. We've gone with the solid 840 EVO from Samsung. If you want to be first to load into your favourite multiplayer map, then solid state is the way to go. Since 250GB isn't going to get you very far we've backed it up with 2 terabytes of more traditional storage for your more pedestrian content.

No gaming laptop can compete with our LAN system in terms of bang for buck.

Alternatively you might be on a budget. Gone are the days when you had to sacrifice power and affordability in favour of a smaller form factor. Take a 1080p gaming experience on the move with this pocket rocket PC.

We've chosen parts that are more than capable of reaching the ever important 1080p at a stable framerate, but we've also opted for hardware that will make this little beast of a machine far more portable. If you anticipate moving your PC often – maybe from the study to the living room, or perhaps regular social LAN events with friends – then this is a highly recommended build to go for. If not then feel free to match many of these parts with a more traditional case; that's the beauty of PC building these days, it's all fairly compatible. This is our cheaper, travel-friendly build.

Here's what we've chosen:

• Bitfenix Prodigy Case	**£70**
• Asus Z97I-Plus Motherboard	**£100**
• Intel Core i5 4690K	**£180**
• Arctic Cooling Freezer 7 Pro Rev 2 CPU cooler	**£20**
• NVIDIA GeForce GTX 960 2GB	**£170**
• 8GB PC3-12800 DDR3 Memory	**£60**
• 1TB Seagate SSHD Hybrid drive	**£60**
• Corsair CX600 PSU	**£60**
TOTAL COST	**£720**

It's *amazing* how much power and flexibility you can cram into a system barely a third the size of a traditional full-tower PC. What's brilliant about the Bitfenix Prodigy case we're using

here is that despite using tiny mini-ITX motherboards, unlike most mini-ITX systems you can fit a full-size gaming-grade power supply (the maximum PSU depth is 160mm) and pretty much any graphics card you care to mention (within reason of course – we hope we don't need to explain why an NVIDIA Titan wouldn't be a good fit).

So how have we managed to build a small-form-factor gaming PC at half the price of our already affordable mid-tower case? Most of it comes down to our sensible choice of CPU and graphics card – the Core i5 processor and GeForce 960 combined cost about the same as the Haswell-E processor from our other system build.

While you'd be forgiven for thinking you're sacrificing too much with an i5 processor you'd be very much mistaken. Many performance benchmarks would show a fairly sizeable gap between this and an i7 in terms of raw number-crunching capabilities, but you'll be hard-pressed to see any difference in gaming performance. Couple this with the fact the i5 4690K is easily overclocked to 4.2GHz with the Asus Z97I-Plus Motherboard and you've got a seriously tasty gaming PC at an unbeatable price.

As for the build itself, well we've arranged it into a fashion that is easier to find the part you're hoping to install. Since all cases and parts are different we can't give you a completely exact run down, but with these steps you'll have no problem tackling whatever situation you find yourself in. We've included the odd alternative option, too, to allow for different case designs that might catch anyone following this process off guard somewhat.

Installing the CPU and RAM

Prepare the motherboard
The worst first move would be to screw your motherboard into the case without first installing two of the most important – not to mention delicate – components of the entire system. Carefully unpack your motherboard from its box. It should have some foam packaging in the box with it; rest your motherboard on it, on a sturdy, well-lit table.

Unlock the CPU socket
There are two levers on either side of the CPU socket; push down and away from the socket on both levers one by one to release them. Pull them up and clear of the socket. This has released the load plate, which in turn can be lifted to free the CPU socket's protective cover. Note the four alignment keys on the naked socket in all four corners and the triangular mark in the top right.

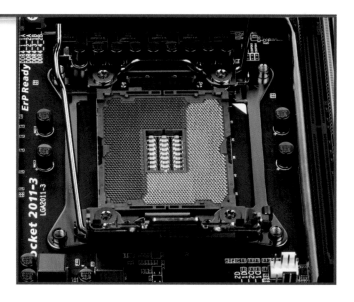

Install the processor

The alignment keys and the triangular mark are mirrored on the processor. Orientate the processor so the triangular mark is in the same place and – without touching the metal contacts on either the processor or the motherboard – gently place the processor into the socket. It will fit very snugly, but if it doesn't appear to be sat correctly, lift it to reposition it (don't be tempted to simply wiggle it around where it lies).

Secure the socket

Once you're happy the processor is sat squarely on the socket, carefully lower the load plate, which is designed to ensure no one side or corner of the processor takes too much pressure when the cooler is installed later on. Next lower and secure the levers on both sides of the processor. It takes a reasonable amount of force so don't be too shy.

Install the memory

The eight memory sockets on this X99 motherboard are divided into four channels, each with two DDR4 slots. Since we're installing 16GB of memory with four 4GB memory sticks, we populate all the grey slots. If we were using two sticks of 8GB we would populate the third and sixth socket. To install each stick, simply line the notch on the memory with the alignment key on the socket. Press down firmly and lock the latches. If you're not installing a separate, dedicated cooler for your CPU then you'll still want to attach the stock cooler that will come with your processor. The instructions may differ for your particular CPU, but in most cases you'll simply remove any protective wrapping, place the cooler on top and push firmly down on the four clips in each corner.

PART # Installing a CPU with dedicated cooler

Prepare the motherboard

If you've decided to install an additional, dedicated fan onto your CPU then there are a few extra steps. Much of the work here will mimic our mid-tower build, starting by laying out the motherboard on its protective wrapping on a clear, flat surface so we can fit the processor. In this example we're dealing with a smaller motherboard in a smaller space, and in this situation the memory will need to be installed later. Raise the locking level on the right of the CPU socket and move the load plate clear.

Placing the processor

Look for the two alignment keys on the socket towards the top of the left and right edges – they match in with the notches on the Core i5 processor. You'll also notice that the triangular key on the processor matches with the socket too. Without touching either the contacts on the socket or on the rear of the processor, carefully orientate and place the processor so it sits snugly in the socket.

Locking the load plate

With the processor in place we can now lower the load plate, removing the black protective plastic before it's locked. Lower the locking lever down and secure it under the locking arm. With that complete we can move on to fitting the CPU cooler – in this case an Arctic Cooling Freezer Pro Rev 2 air cooler. Remove it from its packaging and lay out the Intel socket mounting plate, screws and push-pins.

Fit the Intel mounting plate

Let the mounting plate sit in the four holes that surround the socket on the motherboard. The raised sides with screw holes should be on the left and right as pictured. Drop the beige holders into the corner holes as shown. No pressure or fixings are needed at this point – just make sure they're angled and orientated as shown before moving on to the next step.

Lock the cooler mount

Next you need to place the black push-pins into the beige holders so the flat edges are facing away from the socket and the curved edge is facing inwards as shown. Push them down firmly as far as they go. Once they're all locked in place you can grab the main body of the CPU cooler from one side, but don't fit the fan mount just yet.

Secure the cooler

Remove the protective cover from the heat pipes, revealing the pre-applied thermal paste. Gently sit the cooler on to the CPU socket lining up the screw holes on the mount with the screw holes on the cooler itself. Now securely fasten the cooler to the mount with a cross-headed screwdriver. Next fit the CPU fan connector to the top left of the CPU socket and then gently clip the fan mount to the flat side of the cooler, minding the fins as you go (they're both sharp and delicate).

PART ③ Fitting the motherboard

Prepare the case 1
The NZXT Source 340 case we're using has lots of great PC-building conveniences built into it, but first we need to strip it down so we can start fitting our components. Once it's out of the box remove the two sets of thumbscrews and carefully remove the left and right side panels. The nearside, with the window built in, needs to be carefully protected – it's prone to scratching. Remove the small box of components from the hard-drive rack, as we'll need them shortly.

Prepare the case 2
In this build we need to remove the top panel of the case so we can install the radiator for the water cooler, but this can be skipped if you're not opting for water cooling. The case top panel is only held in place with clips on the front and back, so be brave and give it a sharp vertical tug bearing in mind the front panel connectors for USB and audio are connected to the case itself. Put it carefully to one side.

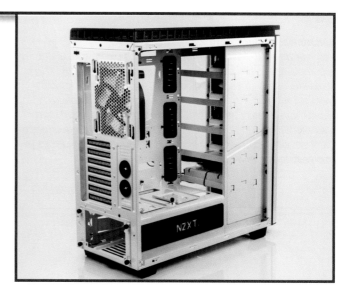

Input/output shield

Next we need to install the motherboard input/output shield, which is designed to show you which connectors serve what purpose on your computer. The keyboard and mouse connectors should be at the top of the rear panel and the audio connectors at the bottom. When you've got it the right way up, push the input/output shield firmly into place so it clips in snugly on all four sides.

Secure the motherboard 1

With the case prepped and the CPU and memory securely installed we can slot the motherboard into the case. While many will prefer to lay the case on its back to place the motherboard over the case screw holes, modern cases have a small stud towards the centre of where the motherboard sits that allows you to hang it in place with the case stood upright.

Secure the motherboard 2

Whichever your preferred method, once the screw slots are positioned over the case riser screws, use cross-headed screws from the box supplied with the case to fix the motherboard securely to the case. It's a very tight fit, which requires some lateral pressure to ensure the inputs and outputs slot through the motherboard back plate. With all screws secure, you can connect the LED cable for the input/output shield – refer to your motherboard manual if you can't find it.

PART Installing horizontally

Strip the case

For smaller cases like this, the motherboard may have to be installed horizontally. Start by removing the two thumbscrews holding both side panels in place and put them both safely to one side. With both side panels removed you can also pop the top panel of the case free too. Remove the cardboard box of components from the hard-drive tray, then slide the entire top hard-drive tray out of the case.

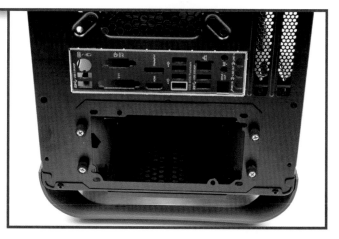

Insert the input/output shield

Find the input/output shield from the box the motherboard came in and carefully push it into the opening just below the rear case fan. Looking from the back the keyboard or mouse connector should be on the left edge and the audio connectors on the right. If you're going to use the Wi-Fi, now is the time to connect the antenna to the back of the input/output shield using the screws provided.

Fit the motherboard

In this situation the motherboard sits directly above the PSU chamber and four screw risers are already in place for it to attach to. Carefully lower the motherboard on to the screws and apply some lateral pressure and ensure the input/output connectors are correctly slotted through the shield. Use the screws provided with the case to fix the motherboard securely in place – they're located in all four corners of the board. Finally connect the rear case fan connector to the motherboard as pictured.

PART 3 Installing both hard drives

1

Remove the SSD tray

Directly under the newly fitted motherboard there are two 2.5in SSD hard-drive bays with removable trays, each secured with a single thumbscrew. Undo the thumbscrew and slide out the tray. Using four small cross-head screws from the components box supplied with the case, carefully secure the SSD drive to the tray as pictured. Be careful not to use the wrong screws, or over-tighten them.

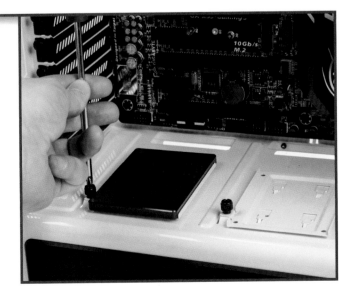

2

Install the SSD

With your SSD drive secured to the drive tray you can slide it back into the case and tighten the thumbscrew to secure it. The drive should be sat 'pretty side up' with the SATA data and power connector of the drive facing towards the motherboard. The cabling for the SSD – and other components – will be coming through the small holes around the motherboard, but first let's spin the case around and install our 2TB 3.5in hard drive...

3

Remove the hard drive rack

Running the height of the front of the case you'll see a number of full-size hard-drive trays. Unlock the thumbscrews of the lowest tray – we're going to use this bay for our 2TB storage drive. Why the lowest bay? It sits in the direct path of the airflow created by the front and rear case fans meaning it'll be actively cooled during use.

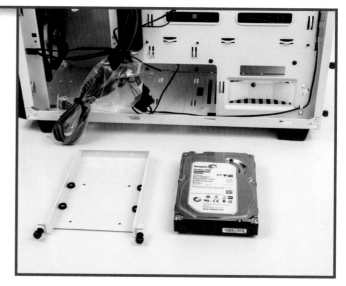

4

Attach the 3.5in hard drive

Next you'll need to screw the hard drive into the tray as you did with the SSD but using the larger screws provided. They're the same size as the screws you used to attach the motherboard to the case. Make sure the drive is really securely fastened: unlike the SSD drive, this one has spinning platters so loose screws can cause noise-inducing vibrations during use.

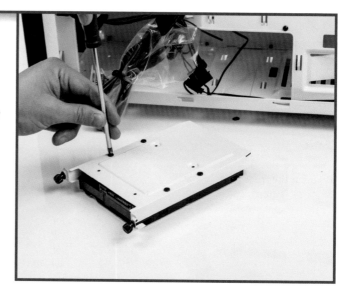

5

Replace the tray

Finally, slide the drive and tray back into the runners it came from. The thumbscrews will need to be tightened by hand but then secured firmly with a cross-headed screwdriver to ensure it's not going to move. Check the unoccupied bays running up to the top of the case and make sure they're tightly fastened too before we start looking at connecting all the core motherboard cables.

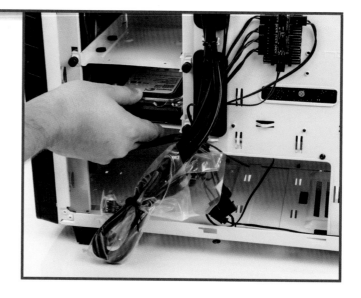

PART Cable routing

Keep your case tangle-free

With some cases you'll see above, below and to the side of the motherboard a number of holes between the motherboard side of the case and the side panel. It's a relatively slim cavity but there is enough room to route most of your gaming PC's cables. It's important to keep as much of the central cavity as free from cabling as possible so cool air has a clean path over your core components. Let's start by feeding through and connecting the cables for audio and USB that sit on the top of the case.

Connect the front panel cables

Since all the connectors for the front panel of the PC run along the very bottom edge of the motherboard we'll bring them through the bottom slots starting with the HD Audio connector that attaches in the bottom left-hand corner. The next slot, for USB 2.0, sits on the right side of the lowest PCIe slot. Further right, under the motherboard chipset block, is where you'll connect USB 3.0, followed by the LED, power and reset connectors. You'll need to refer to the motherboard manual for a connectivity key.

Securing cabling with ties

We've already got a number of cables running around the small cavity on the rear side of the case between the motherboard plate and the side panel, but there are more to come. This being the case, secure the front-panel cables on the metal loops using cable ties, making sure they sit as flat against the case as possible. Try and have the shortest length of cable poking through into the central case cavity to preserve the flow of air through the case from its front and rear fans.

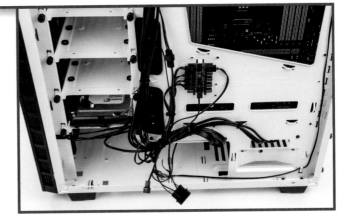

PART **Installing the power supply**

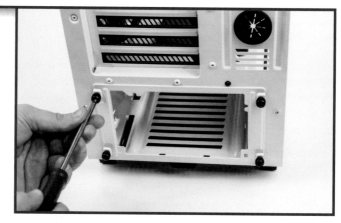

❶ Fix backing plate

Spin the case around to its rear edge. Next we're going to remove the PSU (power supply unit) backing plate from the case using the four thumbscrews pictured. The plate is designed to connect to the power supply itself, before sliding back into the case. With the backing plate removed, unbox your PSU and connect the plate using the four screws.

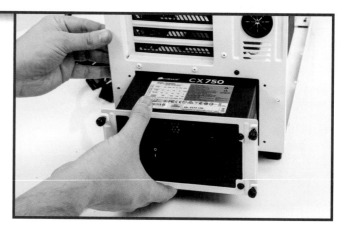

❷ Feed power cables

With the backing plate secure, we now need to gently feed the entire bundle of PSU cables through the hole, pulling them through the side port so there's plenty of room for the PSU to slot into the bay. Tighten the four thumbscrews with a screwdriver and then spin the case around so we can work on the tangle of cables connected to the PSU.

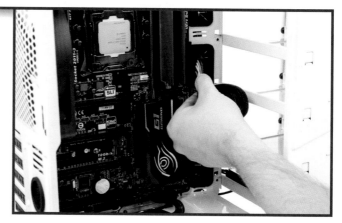

❸ Step 3: Powering the motherboard

First we need to separate the large 24-pin cable and the smaller 8-pin CPU power cable from the PSU cable bundle. We need to feed the larger of the two through the rear side of the case via the middle vertical port so we can carefully twist it round and connect it to the motherboard. Next do the same for the smaller 8-pin CPU-specific power connector, only we need to use the smaller port in the top left corner next to the rear fan.

Connecting the SSD

Now we'll feed the power cable for the SSD through the nearest cable-management port underneath the lowest PCIe slot and connect it to the SSD drive – you might need to unlock it from its tray. Connect a SATA cable to the hard drive and run it through the same hole and around the back of the case. Feed it back through the lowest vertical port and connect it to the top SATA 3 port of the motherboard (port 0).

Connecting your hard drive

The storage hard drive power and data cables can now be connected, but beware: If you're using a motherboard that supports both SATA 2 and SATA 3, you'll need to avoid SATA 2 port 0 for your second 'data' hard drive, or it will clash with your intended boot drive (the faster SSD). Next connect the molex on the back of the case that supplies its many fans and then cable-tie everything in place.

Graphics card power

One of the final PSU-related tasks is to ensure the graphics card has power connectors available for when it's fitted later in the process. The power of your graphics card will dictate whether it needs one or two PCIe power cables fed through the bottom cable port. We're using a pretty high-end card here so we'll need both. Finally (and if they're not removable) cable-tie the remaining PSU cables that aren't in use to the bottom of the case – there's ample room behind the PSU for this.

PART Cable management in smaller cases

Move the cables out of the way

While the PSU cables are the ideal length for full- and mid-tower cases, there's going to be quite an excess of cabling snaking around the inside of smaller cases. Carefully twist and tidy the excess cable length as shown and then connect the 24-pin and 8-pin motherboard cables. It's a good idea to use cable ties where possible to manage excess cabling and it will help secure these larger cables safely.

Smart connections

Regardless of the size of case or the parts you use, it's important to be sensible about the way you connect the different cables. You don't want them to be a mess of wires interweaving with one another, so start in a sensible order and make sure they're connected in an orderly manner.

Cable management

If you are using a smaller case, or have opted for a cheaper case that doesn't feature in-built cable routing options, then you'll also need to make an effort to keep the area around the motherboard – and its connected parts – as free as possible. This is to allow cool air to travel about the system efficiently.

PART **Fit the system panel and memory**

Connect the case-specific cables

Finally turn the case around and bunch up all the remaining cables bar a single PCIe power connector for the graphics card. Cable-tie them neatly to the side of the case. You may wish to use the provided Reset, Power, Power LED and HDD LED connector provided with the case to assist in connecting the system panel connector cable from the side panel. It connects directly to the right of the SATA ports. Drape the cables over the hard-drive rack.

Connect system panel connectors

You'll need to drape the USB and audio system panel connector cables over the hard-drive rack too, since they all connect on the far side of the case. It can be trickier with smaller cases to find the various connections, in our case - for example - the USB 2.0 can be found directly behind the PCI-E slot (for the graphics card), the USB 3.0 connector is directly to the left of the SATA ports and the audio connector is located directly next to the audio output on the rear edge. At this point you should also install your memory sticks, since in smaller cases it can be harder to manage with the RAM already installed (as would be the case in a mid- or full-tower case).

Closing the first side panel

Once you're done with all this you can get the side panel back on. It's not always quite so straightforward, however, because some cases will need you to tidy the side-panel connector cables as best you can, leaving some slack for future access. Once you're satisfied the cables won't impede airflow through the case, push the side panel into place and tighten the provided thumbscrews.

PART Installing a water cooler

❶ Connect the USB 2.0 internal cable

Familiarise yourself with the water cooler and its instructions. Take the internal USB 2.0 cable and connect it to the motherboard on the bottom edge of the board. Feed it out through the bottom cable hole, run it up the back of the case and drop the other end down through the top-left hole ready to connect to the CPU water block when it's ready to be fitted.

❷ Fit the radiator fans

Put the radiator on a table with the water pipes pointing upwards on the right-hand end. Pay particular attention to the image and orientate the fans so their power cables are nearest you. Affix both fans to the radiator with the long screws and washers provided.

❸ Install the mounting bracket

Hand-screw all four double-sided mounting screws designed for your chosen CPU package into the outer four corners of the CPU socket. You can ignore the provided backing plate and the other sets of double-sided mounting screws since they won't be compatible with your particular CPU socket design.

Fit the radiator

The radiator can be quite fiddly to fit single-handed, but with the fans connected and the water pipes facing towards the front of the case, carefully sandwich the radiator to the inside top of the chassis and use the eight screws provided to fit it into place.

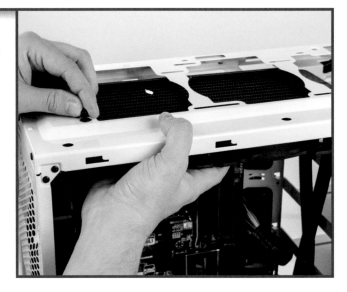

Mount the water block

Connect the provided cables to the water block (the CPU fan, power and two radiator fan connectors) as per the manufacturer's instructions, then fit the compatible CPU mounting bracket using the four thumbscrews to fit the water block over the CPU (thermal paste is pre-applied on the block). Hold it firmly in place while you screw two opposite corners of the block first to ensure even pressure across the CPU socket.

Mount the water block

With the water block securely attached, run the connected cables out through the top port of the case and down the back of the motherboard. The CPU fan connector can be found to the bottom-right corner of the CPU socket and the SATA power connector can be connected to a spare port from the PSU. Finally secure everything with cable ties, ensuring there's ample clearance for the side panel to fit back on (though don't fit it just yet).

PART **3** Fitting a graphics card

Unscrew the PCIe slot covers

The final part of the hardware build process is fitting the graphics card. Since our graphics card is a double-height model we'll need to remove the top two PCIe slot covers with a screwdriver. Carefully unbox your graphics card and remove the plastic protector from the PCIe connector if it has one fitted. Line up the graphics card with the top PCIe slot and slide it in until it clicks into place.

② Unscrew the PCIe slot covers

Once you've replaced the thumbscrews to help support the weight of the graphics card and hold it firmly in place, you can connect the power cables (the GeForce 970 uses both). Make sure the cable clips are facing down and push them both firmly into place until they click. Pull the remaining cable through so it's not too slack and secure to the rear of the motherboard tray.

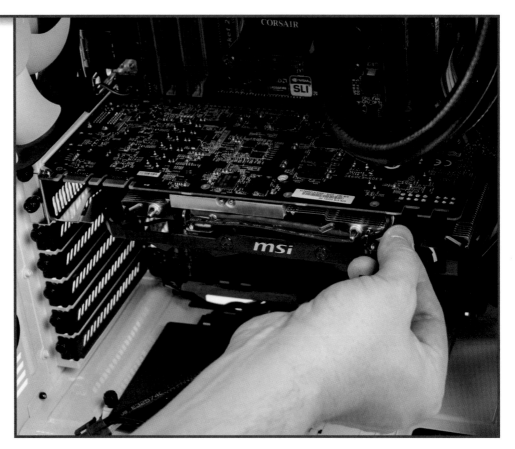

③ Finishing off

Give the inside of your new PC a once-over to make sure everything's connected correctly. You can now replace the side panels and begin installing your chosen operating system, but we'd recommend you try and power up the system before you replace the side panels. If nothing happens, refer to the fault-finding chapter elsewhere in the book and retrace your steps through the build process to confirm everything is connected properly.

4

```
lp
cinnamon-s
cinnamon-sound-a
co
cinnamon-sett
-lock-dialog
int /usr/share/themes $ cinnamon-sett
ress_close() takes exactly 3 argument
gress_close() takes exactly 3 argument
ogress_close() takes exactly 3 argumen
recent call last):
o/cinnamon-settings/bin/ExtensionCore
/cinnamon-settings/bin/ExtensionC
spices()                                          /ExtensionC
lib/cinnamon-settings/bin/ExtensionC
ces.load(self.on_spice_load, force)
sr/lib/cinnamon-settings/bin/Spices.p
refresh_cache()
usr/lib/cinnamon-settings/bin/Spices
load assets()            settings/bin/Spice
lib/cinnamon-settings/bin/Spice
f icon_path)             settings/bin/Spi
n-settings/bin/Spi
aborted.'
```

PART **4** BUILD YOUR OWN GAMING PC

The first start-up

Congratulations! If you've followed our guide then at this point you should have your very own gaming PC put together and ready to go. Well done you. Before you start celebrating too much, however, it's fair to say that much of the work is yet to come. Hopefully you've enjoyed the experience of putting the hardware together, but now the time has come to check the machine works and, if it does, start tinkering with the software side of things. And truth be told, as necessary as it is, that part isn't nearly as fun.

The first start-up of your first ever gaming PC can be quite intimidating; it's the reward for your patience and effort, and if it doesn't boot up it's hard not to feel like something of a failure. But it does happen to the best of us, with common problems such as putting power connections in the wrong place stifling many a would-be powerhouse PC. Fear not, crack open that panel and have a tinker – ensure that the power is taken out, of course – and look for any connections that aren't in the right spot. If needs be, remove the power cable connections and repeat that process for each of the PC's parts in turn, using your motherboard's manual as a reference guide. Each motherboard and case is different, so it could be a simple problem you've overlooked.

But since troubleshooting can be such a large undertaking – especially if it's something greater than a misplaced power connection – we'll focus on that in a separate section later on in the book. Instead this chapter will assume all is hunky dory with your PC build, and will talk you through some of the key facets of your gaming PC post-build. It'll focus on things like installing an operating system, booting up your PC for the first time and some of the first actions you'll want to take. It's your PC, ultimately, so you should feel free to tailor the software to match your interests or personal desires – but we'll guide you through some of the more important gaming software.

The irony is, of course, to install an operating system you'll first need access to another computer. If you can't visit a friend or go to the library then there are ways around this, but we'll talk about all that in this chapter. After everything is installed there's a temptation to jump straight into playing games – and there's certainly nothing stopping you doing that – but with just a little bit extra work you can be completely set up without any concerns that might rear their head because you were overeager in rushing to play games. There are various settings you can tailor to make your gaming PC a truly carefree kit, so we'll detail some of these, too.

Simply put, everything that comes after the hardware installation will be discussed here and so, with only a little bit of extra work, you'll be ready and raring to go before long.

Picking an operating system

We have to admit, these days it can often feel like there aren't many options when it comes to operating systems. So prevalent is Microsoft's Windows OS that it's rare many will even consider other alternatives – but they are there, with some that you might not have considered beforehand.

Currently there are only really three major operating systems: Windows, OS X (exclusively for Apple Mac products) and the open-source Linux. Since you'll be running a PC you won't be able to consider OS X, reducing your core options down to only two. Windows is the safest option of them all; it's not that Linux will cause any problems with your machine, but Microsoft's operating system is stable, relatively hassle-free and will have the widest possible compatibility with games and software. But it will cost you more money, and a licence

Microsoft has been very careful with Windows 10, trying to strike a balance between 'classic' Windows systems and the Windows 8 tiling option.

← Windows 8 had a lot of criticism for making it confusing for users to navigate and utilise, so might not be a good option to go with.

for the latest copy of Windows can add a good chunk on top of your overall budget. To confuse matters a little more, your options for Windows includes version 7, 8 or 10 – the latter of which is the most recent. Windows 7, despite its age, is still a popular choice, it is robust and offers the most typically 'Windows' experience. Windows 8 was criticised heavily upon its release for over thinking that classic design, but it was popular among laptop and tablet users – which is what Microsoft was targeting. Windows 10 is the most modern, having been launched very recently. Looking toward the future, you may want to pick Windows 10 for its consideration of PC architecture more familiar to yours and its enabling of DirectX 12 – but of course it all comes down to cost and personal taste.

Linux is open source, meaning it is free to download and install – a great option if you're looking to save some pennies. But it is worth noting that Linux does come with some issues: for one thing it won't be totally familiar to anyone who has used a PC in the last decade – this isn't Windows and you will need to learn a few things. It also has a number of compatibility issues and while it isn't quite as major an issue as it once used to be there could be concern that something – whether it's specific software you want to use or hardware and their drivers – won't work. It's also worth noting that there are a wide range of Linux distributions or distros – a term used to

↙ Though not officially sold by Microsoft anymore, it's still possible to buy licences for Windows 7, which currently is a popular option for those who want an unobtrusive OS experience.

Valve's SteamOS is fairly new, but offers great integration with its digital distribution platform that most gamers are a part of.

Team Fortress 2
Not installed

PLAY

YOU'VE PLAYED **757 Hours**
LAST PLAYED **Saturday**
STREAM FROM **Martin-PC**

LINKS & MORE

FRIENDS WHO PLAY

WORKSHOP

+135

LT WEB

A SELECT Y MORE WAYS TO PLAY

FRIENDS RT

describe the different 'flavours' of operating system. For each of these Linux remains the foundation, but the creator (or creators) have provided their own preference or spin on things. This can confused matters for those looking for a new operating system, but sticking with the more popular distros – such as Ubuntu or Linux Mint – will minimise any of that hassle.

Then there is SteamOS, an operating system also built on Linux and free to download but designed and produced by Valve, the developers of the Steam software – the number one name in gaming today. It's still early days for the OS just yet so expect it to be fairly low on the number of features, but with already over 1,000 compatible games on Steam – and hardwired integration with your Steam account – it's certainly a good option if gaming is your central reason for building a PC. It's free to download anyway, so give it a try.

Linux is an option for those with a preference for getting stuck into the nitty gritty and don't mind debugging the odd problem that might arise, while Windows will be the better choice for those who just want their operating system to work with as few problems as possible.

Ubuntu is the most popular Linux distribution, and blends elements of Mac OS X and Windows into its own system.

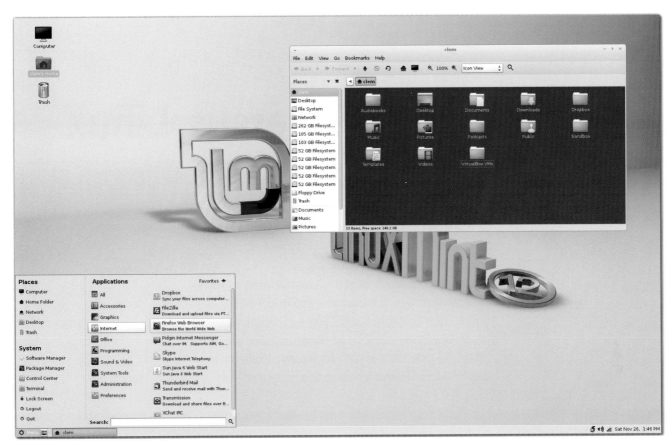

Mint is perhaps the Linux distro that is closest to Windows in terms of functionality and design, and offers a nice, sleek interface.

Since Linux is open source it's possible to really get stuck into customising the operating system to your needs.

PART 4 Windows versus Linux

With a huge majority of the market share, Windows is by far and away the most popular operating system for PCs the world over. What this means is that we're fairly confident that you'll be able to pick up any model of Windows for your PC and have few problems adapting to it – even if you haven't used a PC for five years or more! That's going to take precedence if you're not willing to learn more technical elements, and we'll acknowledge that. However, we wouldn't be doing our job if we didn't at least give you the alternatives. Here's a comparison between Windows and Linux, to find out which is for you.

	Windows	Linux
Price	At a cost of around £100 for the basic licence, and up to £200 or more for more 'professional' packages, the cost of Windows can add a lot to the already expensive cost of your PC. As a general note, pay attention to what you actually get in the upgraded packages; you may find much of the extra software included is not something you'll actually have much interest in. Additionally, if you're a student, you may be able to buy Windows at a discounted price – so look out for that.	Since the majority of Linux distributions are completely free to download, the obvious winner when it comes to price is this operating system. There are many reasons to choose Linux over Windows, and price is a big selling point. It doesn't need to be a permanent choice, either; if you find you don't enjoy using your installed operating system then you can easily switch it out, whether that's for Windows or a different Linux distro. With no cost involved, there's less pressure to force yourself to use it.
Compatibility (Software)	This is the ultimate strength of Windows, at least when it comes to games. With its huge market share, it's unsurprising that developers will first focus on a Windows version of the game, with Mac's OS X coming next and Linux after that. If playing every game as and when they come out is important to you then Windows will likely have to be the choice of OS – it is where the most consumers are, and so it's going to be the first port of call for developers.	Once upon a time Linux struggled when it came to game releases; very few were released on the platform and it was a sore point for many gamers. Nowadays however – as the popularity of Linux continues to rise – it is becoming a much more viable platform for games. It doesn't hold a torch to Windows in this regard – it is said that Linux accounts for roughly 5% of PC game sales – but these days each new release is, for the most part, brought over to Linux. If this release is not simultaneous with Windows, then take comfort in knowing that many games do release for Linux eventually. It's a burden Linux users need to carry, sadly.
Compatibility (Hardware)	We'll be saying this a lot, but Windows is the most popular operating system and so, as a result, it is also more likely to receive driver support from hardware manufacturers. It's unlikely you'll have many problems with your hardware as a result of using Windows.	Manufacturers have made great strides in providing driver support for Linux, and since technical savvy gamers are – by a large margin – some of the more common users of Linux the need to create compatible drivers for specialised PC gaming hardware means it's increasingly less rare to find your hardware supported. It's still worth checking, though, because while your hardware is likely covered it's possible to overlook the specific nature of gaming hardware.

	Windows	Linux
Ease of use	Since Windows is by far and away the most popular platform when it comes to PCs – though Apple Macs are becoming increasingly popular in offices and the like – the ease of use of its software is something that Microsoft has tried to focus on. Most people will know how to use a Windows PC – even with the most basic tasks – and in that regard Windows wins out when it comes to intuitiveness.	Depending on the distribution of Linux that you use, the ease of use with this operating system can vary. The more popular distros like Ubuntu, Mint and Debian all offer a user interface that is very familiar to Windows users, but many of the options and settings are in different places – it won't always be immediately apparent where these can be found and if Windows has been your staple OS for years then you may find yourself having to relearn a bit more than you might have been willing to.
Software	Windows comes with a whole host of extra bits of software – and some would say far too much of it, in fact. In truth there is a lot of bloatware inside even the basic Windows install, but with a number of accessibility and system options available that just have no equivalent in Linux you can be sure that – in terms of sheer number of extra utilities – Windows edges out. But let's not forget that in this day and age there's often a better (and usually free) option somewhere on the internet.	Linux relies on a particular distribution to quantify just how many extra utilities and software packages come bundled with an install. Some are purposefully more svelte in this regard, while others bundle in as much as they can. It all comes down to preference, but the majority of 'essential' utilities are often all there. With Linux, however, since everything is open source it's far easier to install additional utilities and software with very little effort – and in almost all cases, these installs will be completely free.
Performance	Windows is certainly a user-friendly operating system, but it's not exactly quick to use. A fresh install on your brand new PC might seem pretty nippy, but after numerous mandatory updates and behind-the-scenes software running from start-up it soon starts to add up – eventually turning Windows into a very bloated and slow running OS. In this regard a lot of manual maintenance is required to ensure that your PC remains as quick as possible when it comes to running Windows – and that can become tiresome quickly.	By contrast, Linux is fairly quicker to use. It has a smaller CPU demand – on the whole – meaning the operating system itself isn't intruding on your need to navigate the interface, install items or – frankly – run at a steady and reliable pace. It's impossible to objectively compare the two – since elements such as performance are affected as much by the software you install as anything else. Still, Linux – on average – beats Windows when it comes to speed of use, since it has a much lower demand on your system and less of an eagerness for bloatware.
Security	There's something of a curse to being the most popular piece of software; Windows, as you might expect, is a bigger target for virus and malware than its competitors. You should always stay vigilant when downloading software and opening emails – on any operating system – but due to the way Windows handles access to its files and folders it can put you at a bigger risk if you don't have an antivirus program and firewall preventing these threats from coming in.	Security is a major boon to using Linux. You'll of course want to install compatible antivirus and firewall software but at a foundational level Linux distros tend to offer much great security than Windows. Part of this is because Linux isn't nearly as popular and therefore less appealing to those creating viruses, but in addition to this the way Linux handles administration rights (by default all users have restricted access) means that if a virus does manage to get in the damage it can actually cause is lessened.
OS flexibility	Since Windows is a product managed, maintained and sold by Microsoft it is rare that you can have much input over the form, function and control of the different parts of the OS. This is likely to be a minor concern – with a closed platform comes a more reliable piece of software – but know that you'll have much less freedom with Windows installed.	With Linux you not only have myriad choices of which distribution you prefer and want to use, but you have much greater control over the functions of your machine. It requires a greater technical knowledge – or, at least, a willingness to learn – but if you like the idea of being able to control everything in your OS then Linux is the way to go. In fact, if you want to learn all about Linux, you'll even be able to jump in and edit some of code yourself – if you dare. A true techhead's paradise.

PART  Installing the OS

You might be surprised how easy it is to install an operating system. These days it's pretty much a case of getting hold of the files you need, creating what is known as a 'boot disc' then powering up the PC with it available for the BIOS to detect. This could take the form of a CD, DVD or USB. It's likely the latter will be the option you go for, but the process is essentially the same anyway.

For our guide we'll assume that you're going to opt for Windows, since it is the more popular choice and requires the least technical knowledge. Since there are so many distros for Linux it's perhaps better to suggest that, whichever you go for, make sure you follow any supplied guidelines. It'll likely be just as simple, but there are far too many options for us to account for every single eventuality here.

To begin the process of installing the operating system you're going to want to first pick your method, and make sure you have the necessary hardware capabilities to do so; there's no sense preparing a boot disc on CD if you chose not to have a CD drive in your PC build! It's also worth noting that you'll need access to

There will be a waiting period while installing Windows, so feel free to go grab a cup of tea.

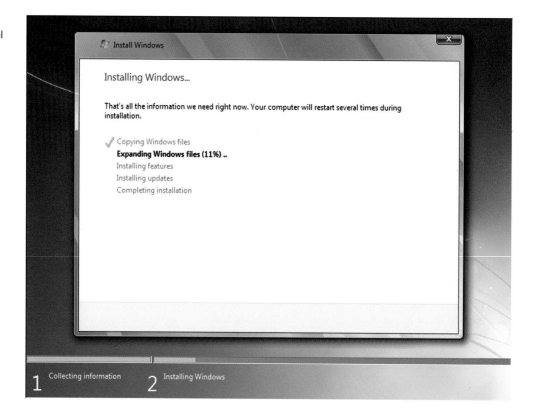

Windows 8 is tied to a Microsoft account – perhaps one you had from Hotmail – and syncs your emails and everything else with it.

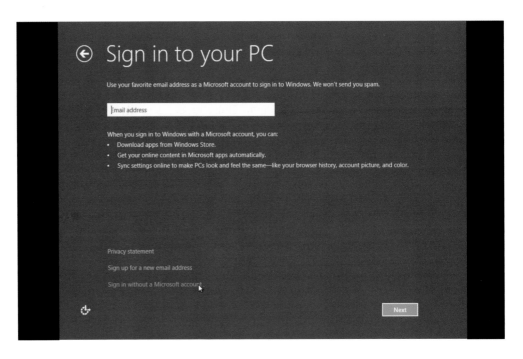

the internet to download the files you need, and understandably without an operating system installed your PC won't yet be ready to do so. See if you can ask a friend if you can borrow their computer, head to the local library and use theirs or maybe even ask the IT guy at the office – you never know, maybe a pleasant smile and a chocolate chip muffin will be enough to persuade him. Anyway, let's get started:

Prepare the boot disc

If you bought a boxed copy of Windows then that's the biggest worry out of the way; it'll come with everything you need, including specific instructions on how to install the software and your associated serial key – go ahead and pop that into your CD drive, you'll be up and running in no time. If you bought a digital version from the Microsoft website – or had to download a bootable disc file since you no longer have your original disc – then that is where you need to actually create the boot disc yourself.

If you're creating your boot disc yourself then you've purchased a digital licence for Windows – it's essentially the same but without the box and removable media. Here you'll be given two options to download, either an ISO file or a collection of compressed files. You're going to want to pick the ISO file, since this will allow you to create the boot disc. With this file downloaded, simply copy it onto a USB or DVD. With a DVD you'll need to make sure the computer you're using allows you to burn DVDs, but in truth you're likely much better sticking to USB anyway – it's quicker, easier and less permanent. Whichever you choose to go for, that's all there is to it – there's your boot disc.

Start the PC up

The next process is simple: either plug in your USB or place the DVD into the DVD tray and then boot up your PC with the power button. We're assuming you've turned your PC on once, at least, so you know it works, so this time around the BIOS will automatically detect the boot disc and prompt you with the following sentence: 'Press any key to boot from CD or DVD/ external device...'

We'll ignore the classic joke about finding the 'any' key; simply press any button on the keyboard and the installation process will begin. You'll need to wait for a little while for the necessary files to be installed. These aren't actually the core operating system files but, instead, the tools to allow for the complete process to be done; the BIOS needs to have something available before it can begin any kind of installation process, after all.

Follow the installation process

From this point on there isn't much more we can tell you. Once Windows is ready to install you'll be greeted with what is known as an installation wizard – or a traditional mouse and keyboard system of steps to help the process along. Regardless of the version of Windows you've chosen you'll be met with a selection of language, date and time and keyboard formats – that's how you know you're ready to properly begin the installation. Though you can change these and any of the following steps once Windows has been installed, it is obviously much more beneficial to pick the choices more relevant to you throughout this process. Simply follow each of these steps and, before too long, you'll be greeted with the desktop of your gaming PC!

PART **4** What software?

So you've put the PC hardware together, you've installed your operating system and now you're looking at your computer's desktop screen. You're done! At this point, providing fire isn't bursting from your fans (honestly, that's not a possibility!) then you're free to do whatever you wish with your computer. If you really want, you can rush off and get some games installed, and test out your build for its graphical capabilities. Every gamer wants to first oggle those polygons, but hold your horses! That is certainly something you could do, but there might be some more setup left to do – in particular, you need to think about some of the important (and not-so-important) software that you want to install first.

When it comes to deciding on what software you want to get, it's important to first think about the things that are imperative to your gaming PC, not only from a security standpoint but also from a gaming standpoint. In this regard antivirus software is just as important as digital distribution outlets such as Steam; it is important to be safe, of course, but how are you planning on

Be careful about where you download files from. Places like CNET can be trustworthy, but you still need to be vigilant about all your software downloads.

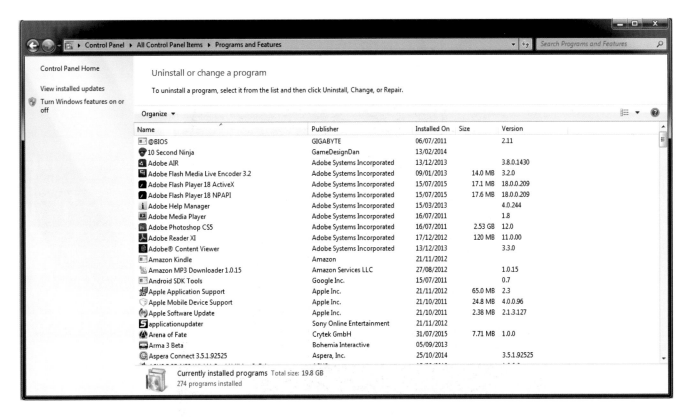

getting access to your games? Steam is the biggest method of buying and playing PC games these days, but it is by no means the only option available – and some would argue not even the best. In this section we'll take a look at all the important pieces of software that you'll need to consider installing early on for your PC, and some of the popular names you'll want to look out for.

There's no ignoring the fact that there is a sheer wealth of software out there available for you to download, and we can't by any means be a complete resource of them all. As with everything in your new gaming PC, think about what it is you want any particular program to do and look for options that best achieve that – it might not be the most popular or even the most reliable, but it might fit you and your needs much better than the more common equivalents. It comes down to smart decisions with informed research, and as long as you download the software from the official page – or something like CNET, which is sort of a resource for this sort of thing – then you can at least feel secure when installing a certain piece of software.

While we're talking about all this, however, it's worth mentioning the importance of tidiness. You'll be surprised how common it is for PC users to install something for a one time use and forget all about it – at best taking up a chunk of your hard drive space, at worst slowing your PC down by taking up CPU processing with behind-the-scenes tasks. Some tools will boot up alongside your PC's start-up, too, and while this is sometimes unavoidable – most gaming keyboards and mice come with bespoke software, for example – an overload of start-up software can put an early task on your CPU that will slow it down for that session. Be vigilant about how much you install, what you do choose to install and – if you know you won't use a piece of software again, or for a while – don't be afraid to uninstall it to keep your PC feeling fresh. A tidy hard drive is an efficient hard drive.

Don't be afraid to regularly visit the Programs and Features section of Windows Control Panel to remove unwanted software.

PART  # Picking a browser

The first thing you'll likely want to install onto your PC is a browser. Now, if you've installed Windows, then the chances are you've already got one installed: Internet Explorer. This is sufficient for getting the job done, but in truth there are so many more options available that it has, depending on who you're talking to, become rather redundant. By all means give it a trial run, but if you ever fancy trying out something else then there's a great number of options out there. For some, Internet Explorer – even with the notable improvements of version 11 – has little other use than to open once to search for (and download) a better alternative.

But what alternative should you go for? Well, that's a tough question and, as with everything here, it'll come down to preferences and needs. Though there are many more out there, the usage market is largely shared between roughly five key competitors, and a large portion of that is thanks to particular operating systems coming with these browsers pre-installed onto their computers; some people don't even realise there are better choices out there. OS X users, on Apple computers, are still making Safari a relevant piece of software, even though it is by far and away one of the worst browsers available. Remember that when looking into your browser of choice: not all users will even be aware of choice.

Internet Explorer will come pre-installed with Windows and can't be fully removed. Don't be afraid to use it to find a better browser

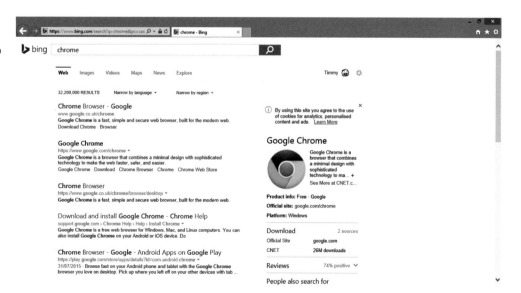

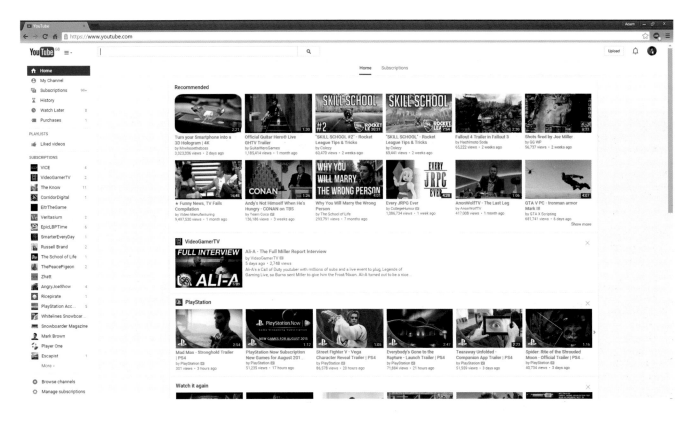

Google Chrome

Google managed to dominate the market a few years ago when it released Chrome, a browser that was sleek, free of clutter and quick. Things have changed somewhat and there's no denying that Chrome's dominance of the market is at risk, but it still remains one of the best browsers out there. It's worth noting that of the major browsers available, Google Chrome is far more intensive on your RAM than it really ought to be. Don't read too much into that though; yes it can cause older computers to slow down if you open too many tabs or windows, but on your gaming PC you will have absolutely nothing to worry about. It's a very feature-heavy browser these days, however, with many important options to make your internet browsing experience a doddle.

Chrome is the most popular browser at the moment, providing a great number of features with a speedy browser.

Positives	Negatives
Sleek and clean interface by default, leaving you with just the websites you want to view and little else. Incredibly fast, too.	More RAM intensive than other browsers, and can cause stability issues when multiple tabs are open.
In-built features such as a spellchecker, incognito mode and website translation options – powered by Google Translate, of course – make it a very user-friendly piece of software.	A minimal interface means many options and shortcuts are hidden behind often confusing menus.
Unresponsive sites won't crash the whole browser software; Chrome lets you safely browse multiple tabs without worry that one site's issues will affect your whole experience.	Though rare, some incompatible or missing software elements require downloading apps – and those apps might not be reliable or even available.
The browser bar acts also acts as a Google search bar – making searching for something even quicker.	Password manager was found to be insecure; so it's best to avoid using it.
Can download apps and add-ons to improve your experience, enhancing browser usage or even pairing up with your mobile phone's equivalent.	

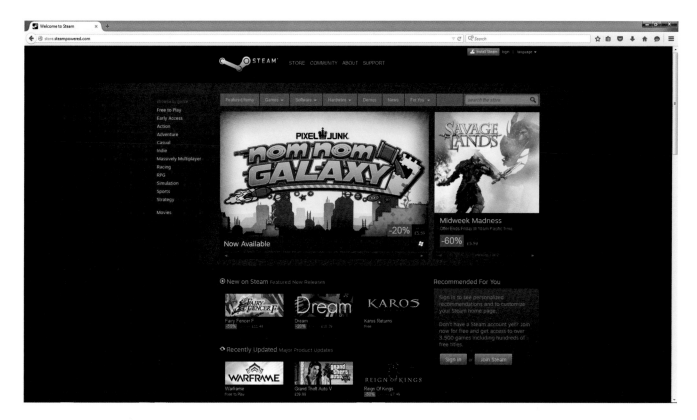

Firefox is well known for its number of additional extras you can download and install onto the browser.

Mozilla Firefox

Before the days of Google Chrome, Firefox was the software to beat. It was almost always the go-to option for anyone looking to ditch the immeasurably worse Internet Explorer. These days it hovers comfortably in second place, behind Chrome, but still maintains a loyal fanbase of users. The biggest selling point for Firefox is its extensions – a means of downloading user-created add-ons that make the browser better in some way. While Chrome now manages the same, Firefox maintains it as a core feature, meaning there are many more options available to would-be users. If you're after a browser that can be customised to your own needs, then Firefox manages a greater level of freedom in that regard.

Positives	Negatives
Regardless of your needs, Firefox has a wide range of extensions available to download and install on to your browser.	Very update-heavy, regularly asking you to update to the latest version.
Very fast browser that doesn't leave you waiting for websites to load – beyond an internet bandwidth limit, of course.	Can crash from time to time, often causing you to lose any searches you might've made.
Features a minimalist interface, and can be more easily customised to include elements important to you – such as bookmarks.	While not quite as bad as Chrome (at times), Firefox can also be quite demanding on system memory.
User security is of utmost importance for Mozilla, and does not make money off user search data – which is obviously unavoidable if you use Google Chrome.	

Opera

Opera has had a mixed history, but these days it's a very commendable browser. It's speedy with a pleasantly clean interface and comes with a selection of unique features. Elements such as widgets – like extensions but with greater interactivity – or speed dial, for opening favourite websites quicker than ever, really help it stand out. It's also got a great deal of flexibility to it, with a number of behind-the-scenes features that could well sell the browser to you. Its quick preferences and session saving features, for example, are subtle extras but might well be enough to make it stand out as your go-to browser.

Opera is still low on the market share scales, but it's a great – and quick – browser that you should at least give a try.

Positives	Negatives
Lightweight browser, low on memory usage and file size and quick as a result.	Not incredibly popular, so website compatibility is often low on the list for web developers to check – sometimes leading to incompatibility errors.
Currently the fastest browser available, albeit only minutely.	Fewer extensions and add-ons to install to alter and improve your browsing experience.
More easily configured than Google Chrome, making it easier to make your own.	Compared to Chrome and Firefox, Opera is lacking in a number of features, making it feel like it is missing important pieces.
Large number of unique features to make it stand out from many other browsers, such as interactive widgets and quick dial web page opening.	

PART  Antivirus and security

With the browser out of the way you can then look to perhaps the most important piece of software you could ever download: antivirus. Sad as it is to say, but Windows PCs often find themselves victims of computer viruses and malware, digital pieces of code or software that look to sneak onto your PC, infect it and cause all sorts of trouble – ranging from CPU or memory issues to wiping important system information stored on your hard drive. It's an easily avoidable problem, however, and so long as you maintain up-to-date antivirus and firewall software and avoid visiting suspicious websites or downloading potentially harmful files then you likely won't ever get struck by such a devastating attack. Just keep an eye out for important changes in the antivirus world; thankfully decent software will automatically alert you to any concerns.

And as with all of the most important software you can download, there are myriad options available. It can be overwhelming, in fact, especially

Good antivirus software quietly keeps itself up-to-date without ever interrupting your PC usage until something is detected.

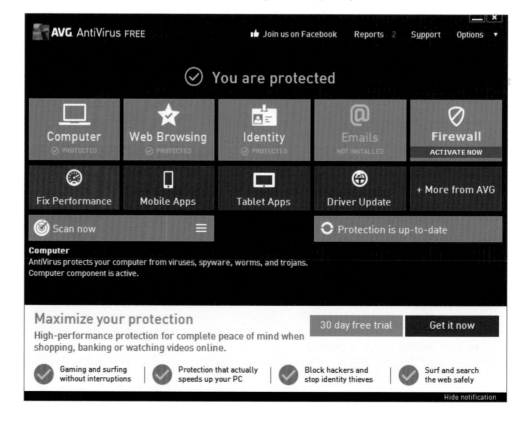

Here's an example of what you can hope to get from free packages when compared to more premium ones.

	Essential Free Antivirus	All-inclusive Internet Security	Top-notch Premier
	FREE DOWNLOAD	DOWNLOAD Free 30-day trial	DOWNLOAD Free 30-day trial
Intelligent antivirus & anti-malware Detects threats no one has even heard of yet.	•	•	•
Home Network Security Scan your home network for weak spots.	•	•	•
Browser Cleanup Get rid of annoying browser add-ons.	•	•	•
Pay & bank online. Safely. Prevent your logins and passwords from theft.		•	•
Anti-hijack protection Log in to your real banking site, not a fake one.		•	•
Silent Firewall Shield your computer from hackers.		•	•
Anti-spam Keeping your inbox junk-free feels good.		•	•
Automatic patching of security holes Reduces the risk of your apps getting hacked. A lot.			•
Prevent misuse of your private data Deleting is not enough. Start shredding instead!			•
	FREE DOWNLOAD	DOWNLOAD Free 30-day trial	DOWNLOAD Free 30-day trial

for antivirus software. It seems these days there are as many antivirus programs as there are viruses! The big names like Norton, AVG or Avast are the more popular, consumer versions but then there are the likes of McAfee, Trend or Bitdefender who might not maintain as wide a portion of the market but offer incredible – and perhaps even better – defence against a range of potential threats.

Rather than give a rundown of specific software brands and models – since there really are far too many – it's perhaps better to discuss some of the important things you need to keep an eye out for, so that you can make an informed decision about which to go for. As with all these things, be sure to check out reviews for any antivirus program you use to get a sense of how safe it will keep your PC.

Pricing

The biggest concern for you will be the question of just how much is antivirus software going to cost? Well, in truth, it needn't cost you anything at all. While PC stores are regularly pitching you an all-in-one protection package from the likes of Norton – often at an annual subscription cost – it's good to remember that cost doesn't always relate to better protection. In fact, with numerous free packages available it's unlikely you'll find a paid-for package that offers much more anyway.

If you have decided to pay for antivirus software, however, make sure you understand what it is you're actually paying for. Many providers will give you little more than a free trial, one that usually lasts little more than 30 days of protection before they chase you for payment – perhaps even locking you out of any security it might've provided. In addition to that, most big-brand antivirus software comes with different tiers of packages – some greater than others. We'll discuss this in more detail below, but make sure that you know the package you're paying for is sufficient for your needs.

The right package

There are a wide range of potential threats to your PC, and the ways in which they attack all differ from one another. Antivirus is just one breed of security software and though it is commonly used as a catch-all name for digital protection from harmful threats, often software comes with different packages to better tailor the safety needs of your PC. If you're fairly vigilant about the websites you visit then you likely won't have much desire for the deluxe packages, since antivirus software will often do enough to protect you from any would-be threats.

Then there is malware, harmful software that sort of tricks its installation onto your system in any number of ways. Windows has in-built protection against such threats, but it is by no means comprehensive, and easily ignored at a human level. Many antivirus programs include protection against malware, too, but it is definitely worth making sure your software of choice comes with such a feature.

Then there's firewall protection; this is a sort of last line of defence against the invisible attacks of the internet, and again Windows has its own secure, in-built software to protect you

Even the most popular antivirus software will try to get you to pay, but you can find completely free options.

from this. If your chosen software comes with its own firewall protection, however, then you can consider switching off Windows' own (sometimes the two can counteract one another) in favour of a more professional one.

System scanning is another common feature, too, though this can take a number of forms. Having a set of tools to detect and eliminate any threats that do get through is important, and it's good to have a scheduled scanner going. Features that allow you to scan your webmail – such as Hotmail – can be very useful too.

Outside of that there isn't really much more you absolutely need your security package to include, but there are a huge selection of extras you could hope to benefit from. Password managers are useful since they will enable you to use a wider selection of passwords for different websites and accounts without having to memorise them all. Automatic updates aren't imperative to the software you choose, but it's much more preferable to the regular reminders or – worse still – no reminders at all, leaving your PC unprotected from new threats.

Efficiency
Though it's less of a concern for someone with a gaming PC – it's kind of a given that you have the CPU and RAM capabilities to run software in the background – it's important to take note of how 'heavy' a footprint your antivirus software will have. Though it's harder to track down that information, reading reviews will often highlight both how quickly any given software can detect threats and also how much of an effect it will have on your processor and memory. This is software that you actually do want to run behind the scenes for as long as your PC is switched on, so knowing it won't eat up too much of your computer's processing power to do that is an added benefit. Be sure to check out the antivirus labs, where you can find out precisely which AV software provides the best protection for the smallest cost on your system.

PART 4 Steam and digital distribution

You may already have noticed how PC games have been taking increasingly smaller parts of many retail outlets over the years, with some even getting rid of them entirely. The reasons for this – while numerous – are primarily down to the cultural importance of digital distribution, or a means by which you buy and own licences to your games but have no physical copy with which to store and install from. Over the years digital distribution has grown and grown to a point where it is now more common to purchase a PC game digitally than to head into a store, pick up a copy and install it onto your computer. As a result, you're going to want to know what your options are when buying a game online.

A large reason for digital distribution's popularity lies in the benefits it offers for everyone involved. Gamers can get immediate access to their library without the need for swapping discs, with only a need to wait for a download to finalise. In most cases updates can be automatically downloaded, too, meaning that any issues that the developer has sought to fix – or even new content that has been added to the game – is ready for you the moment it's needed. On the publisher side of things, it cuts down on piracy – a factor that was a big problem in the earlier days of PC gaming and one that is much harder to overcome when, in most cases, you'll need an account to attribute any download to. It means that publishers can overlook elements like DRM (Digital Rights Management) software that can often cause issues with your PC as it ensures your copy of the game is legitimate, and therefore can leave such invasive tactics out of the game's code completely. If you buy a PC game from a store, it may still contain such software – or it may not contain a disc at all, and instead simply provides a key code to redeem on Steam.

Speaking of which, it's worthing noting that while Steam is the key player in the digital distribution market, there are other alternatives and more are appearing all the time. We'll talk about some of the more important digital distribution software in this section, weigh up the pros and cons, and provide you with reasons to use various means of buying your digital games. But remember, there's no need to tie yourself to any one system; while having your library of games all in one location can be handy, the freedom of choice will give you a much wider selection of software and prices.

Valve introduced a number of methods to help you find games that you might be interested in, adapting its store front around your gaming interests and habits.

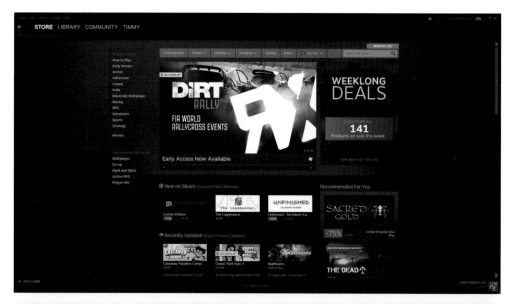

For many the real benefit of Steam is having all your games easily accessible from one location.

Steam

For a long time Steam was the only significant digital distribution option available on PC. Released alongside Half-Life 2 (and the software was mandatory to play the much anticipated game), Steam has grown over the years to become the number one option for PC gamers. You'll need a Steam account and the software itself to buy and install any games, but you can browse a website version of the software or even sign in on a separate app for iOS and Android.

The software itself has a large number of features, such as being able to connect to friends with the in-built social functions or unlockable Achievements as you play to get the most from your games. There is also the Steam Workshop, too, a system built into the program that can help you get even more out of your games. Modding – where gamers alter and improve certain games by creating and releasing downloadable add-ons, or mods – used to be a very separate side of PC gaming, but now with Steam Workshop it has become much more accessible and user friendly. It has its issues, but is a great added feature for those

who want to get the most out of their games. In some cases it has even overtaken outside modding communities, meaning that you may well need Steam if you want to add mods to your game.

Steam is particularly well known for its sales, too, though that is also true of many other digital outlets. Most games launch on Steam with a temporary discounted price, while constant daily and weekly deals mean you can often find games – or entire collections of a series – at a fraction of the usual price. Steam's seasonal sales have become something of a celebration for gamers, too, with numerous games on sale often for little more than a couple of quid.

If this all sounds too good to be true, well, don't worry too much – there is a reason Steam has become the de facto option for so many people. It is worth noting that Steam is a closed system, however; this means you can only access your games by opening the Steam program, and will need to go through various hoops to be able to play them offline. It's enough to put off a number of people, and if erratic internet access might be a problem for you, it might be worth considering the alternatives.

GOG.com

Standing for Good Old Games, GOG's heritage lies primarily in the ability to download older PC games for modern hardware, many of which would be deemed 'classics' by today's standards. While you probably didn't build your super powerful gaming PC to be able to play games from 10, 15 or even 20 years ago, it's worth knowing that this website exists if you are hoping to look for a place to buy and play older titles.

However GOG is still relevant for modern games, too. More recently GOG has begun moving into more up-to-date releases, and in most cases any major release on Steam will get an equivalent release on GOG. Moreover, the website recently released GOG Galaxy, its own take on the Steam software that is intended to give the same persistent library access as Valve's program but with a much greater level of freedom. GOG has always strived to be DRM-free with all of its available software, meaning you don't have

to validate your purchase each time you boot it up. Whether it's through the website or the Galaxy software, you're free to download and install any software you buy off GOG knowing that there won't be any sort of digital rights management imposed on you.

The software itself is a little more simple and includes fewer features than Steam, but it's also much newer software. It still maintains software updating – a necessary feature for modern games – and includes important extras such as social options and in-game unlockable Achievements, though of course you will need to be online for that. However, it's all optional, and this alone is making GOG Galaxy an important competitor to Steam for many gamers. Its openness about software and insistence on DRM-free games does mean that it will come up against resistance from some publishers – so you may not see certain games ever release on GOG – but for the most part it is a great alternative to the powerhouse that is Steam.

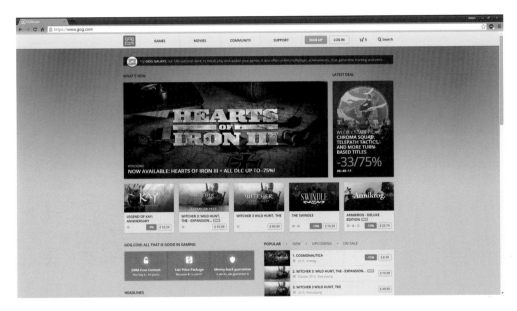

DRM-free is an important motto for GOG.com, so you can download installation files without having to install horrible DRM check software.

The GOG Galaxy software is already in great condition for such an early attempt at taking on Steam.

Green Man Gaming

As with GOG.com, Green Man Gaming – or GMG – started out as just a website selling digital codes for games. Over the years it has grown into the second most popular digital retailer for games and has expanded to include its own software client – Playfire – to install and run a library of games. Cheap prices is something GMG focuses on, however, and with numerous deals and savings regularly throughout each month it's certainly a place you'll want to bookmark to visit regularly.

It's worth noting that its Playfire software isn't the most useful. The large majority of games on GMG's store are actually provided as a Steam code, and while it does mean that you'll sometimes get these games cheaper as a result it is hard to overlook the fact that it is – essentially – acting as a middle man. There are

games that are compatible with Playfire, but those are few and far between and very rarely are they the major releases. It comes with some extra features, however, such as a Rewards system that earns you credit for playing the games you buy. It's a novel method that earns you extra points that can be spent on anything on GMG's website.

Whether or not you opt to use the Playfire software and features, however, it's worth considering for the long-term benefits. Additionally the website is a good alternative to purchasing digital codes – as is Amazon's Digital Store – that will ultimately lead you back to Steam, but often at cheaper prices than otherwise. It is a growing website and set of services, too, which can only mean GMG will more likely solidify its own software as a true Steam competitor in the future.

GreenManGaming offers great benefits for gamers looking to save money, or earn points for money off.

The Playfire software is still very basic, but it'll no doubt grow over the years to something integral to gaming.

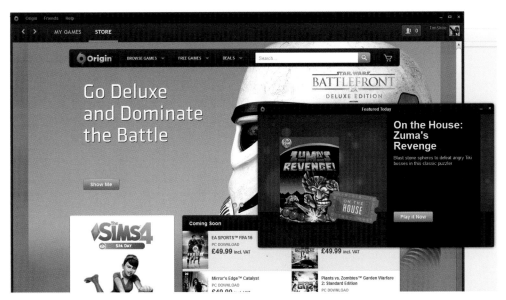

EA often give away some older games completely free as a means of enticing players to actually use their distribution platform.

You'll mostly only use Origin to access EA's games, since they can be quite restrictive about where their games appear.

Origin, UPlay and the rest...

There are countless other places to buy your games digitally these days, whether it's the likes of Gamersgate, Amazon Digital or the charitable (and cheap) collections from Humble Bundle, but regardless of where you shop many of these places just offer a cheaper alternative to Steam, ultimately selling you a key that can then be redeemed on Valve's system. If these websites advertise a 'third-party DRM' then it's either a code for Steam or a separate patcher/installer that you'll first need to use before the game will launch.

It's worth noting at this point that some games – even some on Steam – will require a patcher first. Something like *League Of Legends*, any Blizzard game such as *World Of Warcraft* or *Hearthstone* or the likes of *Elite: Dangerous* will first have to go through separate patchers; since these games are driven by online play there's a need to keep the game up-to-date. If an incompatible version was to connect to an updated server, it could play all sorts of havoc with the software. So some games

– regardless of where you buy them – will still have their own launchers to first check the version of the game you're on and, if necessary, update it.

Besides that we should also point out Origin and UPlay. Both are separate pieces of software controlled by publishers (EA the former, Ubisoft the latter) and act as an arbitrary barrier to entry for many of the publishers' games. They have since learnt that no one likes having to be forced to use their software and so you'll likely find their games also on Steam and elsewhere (and usually cheaper, too), but every so often you will find you may need to download them to play a particular game. As with any other digital retailer they do sometimes have deals or special offers and giveaways, but since this is the 'source', so to speak, don't expect too much in the way of special treatment as a consumer. The software itself is entirely forgettable, too, providing just the very basics necessary to maintain a presence, but not enough that you'll be glad you installed it. If you want our advice, avoid installing Origin or UPlay for as long as you absolutely can.

PART

Social software, and the rest...

What use is your super-powered gaming PC if you can't share it with anyone? Multiplayer gaming has risen to become a significant aspect of the industry, with even most single-player, story-focused games coming with a competitive or cooperative online option too. And sure, while the majority of these modes can be played solo, joining in with a random selection of players through various matchmaking services, there's no denying that the thrill of playing with people you actually know is all the more rewarding – win or lose. Even more besides, whether you want to play with your friends or not, having a means to talk and share your gaming experiences with other people will be imperative to making the most of your PC.

We'll assume you'll be installing Steam – its pervasiveness across the industry is hard to ignore – and that's certainly a great way to keep in touch. The in-built social features of Steam let you add friends, chat with them – both during and outside of a game – as well as set up a public profile for others to check out, and maybe add you. But it is only one system, and functions only within itself. Just as if you were playing *World Of Warcraft* or *League Of Legends* – which also include social and chat features – you're only going to be in touch with friends that are both online and actively playing those games. How would you organise a different game if they didn't know you were online?

As such there are plenty of extra options on top of the in-built, closed nature of many other games and platforms. While they are all utterly optional – which is to say superfluous to your gaming PC's use – you may well find they are among some of the most important pieces of software you will install.

Outside of that there are a lot of other smaller pieces of software that are important and will have some use to you over the course of your general PC use. As such we've created a final table to collate all of the important social and non-social software to help you get a better grasp of the things you should look for and download, or as a reference to return to should you find you suddenly have need for such programs.

Software	Use for...	Details
Raptr	Connecting with your friends.	Raptr supports a wide range of accounts across a number of platforms, and provides a great way to connect to friends outside of specific platforms. Also provides performance boosts for your PC.
Dropbox	Sharing files.	There are multiple cloud storage options, but if you find yourself commonly sharing files then a shared Dropbox among friends will be very useful.
7-Zip	Extracting and compiling groups of files.	7-Zip features the widest range of compatible compile-file types, so it's likely if you come across anything other than a .zip file you'll have use for this. The .7z can only be opened by this software.
WinRAR	Extracting and compiling groups of files.	The alternative option for extracting and compiling files, WinRAR is always active and doesn't require you to open a separate program to use it. Though its range of compatible files is wide, there are some it cannot handle.
VLC	Video playback.	There are a wide number of video file types, and even among the most popular a number of different codecs to run them; VLC will run them all with its very lightweight, simple software.
KeePass	Password management.	To ensure that all your online accounts are secure, consider downloading KeePass to keep your passwords safe, secure and easily referenced. Allows you to use multiple different passwords without having to memorise them all.
Skype	Connecting and speaking with friends.	Skype is not a svelte piece of software and can take up a lot of memory and CPU resources, but has instant message features, is widely used outside of gaming and can be useful for smaller groups of friends.
TeamSpeak	Speaking with a group of friends.	Allows a huge number of users (512 on non-commercial, non-profit servers) that can each be arranged by groups. Very specialised, but just as useful among smaller groups.
Mumble	Speaking with a group of friends.	Open-source software so is completely free to download and use. It is particularly lightweight with high-quality audio, making it one of the more popular voice chat options.
Ventrilo	Speaking with a group of friends.	Allows servers for up to eight people to connect to for voice chat, with rented servers allowing up to 400 connected players. Popular among those who play massively multiplayer games.
CCleaner	Cleans all areas of your computer.	Great software for an older gaming PC, allowing you to clean away unneeded files and folders created as part of your general PC use.
OBS	Streaming your gameplay.	Livestreaming has become a big factor of PC gaming, and OBS is a free piece of software that is both lightweight and feature rich. One of the best options for streaming your gameplay onto places like Twitch.tv and YouTube.
qBittorrent	Download BitTorrent files.	Some games – particularly large online games like MMOs – allow the option to download official game files via BitTorrent, a quicker method of data transfer.
GIMP	Image editing.	Free PhotoShop alternative that includes many of the important features of the paid-for equivalent, including layer and layer masks.
Adobe PDF	Open and view PDF files.	There will be a time where you need to open a PDF file, whether for gaming or not. There are many alternatives, but Adobe's own PDF viewer is a fine option.
SumatraPDF	Open and view PDF files.	As an alternative to Adobe's own software, Sumatra is the most popular free equivalent. Doesn't run in the background, includes numerous options and is very quick to use.
LibreOffice	Create and edit text, spreadsheet and Powerpoint files.	While Microsoft Office is the most popular option for businesses, LibreOffice provides the same features for free. These days, there's no need to pay for an office suite of software.
HoneyView	Image viewer.	The basic image viewing software as part of Windows is fine, but HoneyView is much quicker, sleeker and is compatible with many more file types.
Foobar2k	Audio player.	If music is important to you, Windows Media Player is not software you want to use. There are plenty of free options available, but Foobar2k is the most popular these days. Quick and light software.
iTunes	Manage media files.	While we would never condone using iTunes – as a piece of software it is horrific and intrusive – sadly it's a necessity if you own an iPod, iPad or iPhone.

5

PART 5 Accessories

When putting together the perfect gaming PC it's easy to overlook the importance of all the extras that go with it. When you're throwing half your budget into the graphics card, it's understandable that you might reconsider the amount you're willing to spend on the accessories and peripherals – and when there's as much choice as there is it's often easier just to go for the simplest option. But remember this: while the hardware inside your PC might be core to making your gaming experience technically flawless, the accessories you use will factor in just how comfortable your gaming can be.

Razer manufactures a wide range of PC accessories – everything from mice and keyboards to headsets and gaming controllers.

Take, for example, something as simple as a mouse. Sure you can pick a cheap gaming mouse and it does the job, it moves the cursor around and that's all you need, right? But what about its DPI or in-built acceleration? What type of sensor does the mouse have and does it have the right number of additional buttons? Even the shape of it and its ergonomic design will play a huge part in how useful that mouse is for gaming. It's a surprisingly convoluted process to pick out the right tool for the job, and the same goes for keyboards and headsets and even added extras like racing wheels and joysticks. The games you enjoy playing will directly affect not only the peripherals you need to buy, but what features you need to look for from each of them.

And that's still overlooking the confusing world of monitors, which ranges from the cheap-and-cheerful HD LCD displays to the high-end, super-fast refresh rates or the perfect colour reproduction with the likes of IPS panels. If you thought mice were overwhelming then you've yet to experience the trials that come with buying the right monitor for gaming. We've broken down each of the accessories into the key facets you'll need to consider for the optimum gaming experience, deciphered the marketing babble that comes with them and given you the necessary information to know that the choice you go for is the right one. We've even bundled in a few suggestions of our own, though don't let that be the deciding factor; when it comes to PC peripherals and gaming it's all down to what you need, and that changes from person to person.

In addition to that we've also included a couple of extra sections that technophiles will really appreciate. Oculus Rift is the name on everyone's lips these days after Facebook bought out the company, and if you're interested in experiencing the next generation of virtual reality, this is a gadget you really need to check out. We've broken down the technology inside a Rift headset, and showcased some of the games you ought to try out in the compelling new world of VR gaming. Outside of that there's also a look at NVIDIA's new SHIELD range, an Android-driven pair of devices that lets you play your controller-enabled PC games without having to sit at your desk. Whether you're lounging around in the living room or out and about, SHIELD will let you access your PC games wherever you are through its cloud-based streaming functionality. So from the necessary extras in the form of the ubiquitous mouse and keyboard, or embracing new technologies, this chapter will make sure you always make the right decision when it comes to PC gaming accessories.

PART ⑤ Gaming mice

The problem with mice – especially for gamers – is that what makes the 'best' mouse is, in a lot of ways, completely subjective and really comes down to what it is you want to get from the peripheral. Every PC needs one, obviously, but if you play a lot of MMOs over shooters then the features and benefits that you're looking for from a mouse will vary quite dramatically. The shape of it, how it 'fits' in your hand and even the weight are a big deal when looking for the one that is right for you; it's important to have a think about what it is you need from a mouse before even beginning to look for one to buy. On the plus side it's not entirely mandatory that your choice has all the bells and whistles – a basic option will, for the most part, work just as well as its competition. And since the majority these days are USB-powered, plug-and-play mice, you don't need to worry quite so much about compatibility.

What to look for

DPI – This is the measurement that you're going to encounter a lot when looking at purchasing a mouse. This stands for dots per inch, less often referred to as the more technically accurate CPI, or counts per inch. The higher the DPI the 'quicker' it will read your movements, essentially meaning that you'll need to move the mouse less to get the same responses of a lower-DPI mouse. Thankfully most modern gaming mice will allow you to tweak the DPI settings, while others even feature activated precision modes – whereby a button on the mouse will drop the DPI to get that precision, allowing you to quickly un-toggle once more.

Sensors – Ye olde trackball mice are something of an antiquity these days, with gaming mice instead using two types of sensors: optical and laser. The former uses an LED light and a sensor camera to track the movement, and is better at maintaining response when lifting the mouse or using it on an uneven surface. Laser mice are more common for gaming, though, and enable much better precision with much less jitter (or the misreading of a surface). Of the two you'll likely want to go with laser.

Acceleration – Most mice will have some form of acceleration, a feature whereby the cursor will move faster the faster you move the mouse itself. It can be beneficial in some circumstances, such as if you have a smaller mouse mat or desk space to enable smaller movements of the mouse itself. However, acceleration is generally disliked by many gamers since it means you're not getting the exact one-for-one control over the cursor and means there's an element of unpredictability about cursor movement. It's unlikely it'll be too heavy-handed in gaming mice, and can usually be disabled.

Extra buttons – Every mouse will have at least two buttons, and in all likelihood a clickable scroll wheel, too. When it comes to gaming you're going to want at least a couple of extra buttons built into the mouse itself for that extra speed and efficiency when playing. MOBAs like *League of Legends*, for example, rely on fast reactions and the quicker you can pull off that clutch manoeuvre the more of an advantage you will have. The games you play will affect how many buttons you might need – MMO players will likely want a higher number on their mouse – but it's about finding a balance between comfort and usability and the advantage extra buttons bring.

Mouse suggestions

Roccat Kova+

RRP: £44.99
If you're not looking for any fancy extras then the Roccat Kova+ is your best option. It has a very impressive build quality, lovely matte design and four extra, easily accessible buttons (two on either side) making it very useful for *League of Legends* or *Dota 2* players. Its design is balanced so both left-handed and right-handed players can use it. It often sells for much less than its RRP too, making it a great inexpensive option for LANs.

Razer Naga

RRP: £79.99
Razer has its hands dipped in a wide range of peripherals, but its mice are usually the ones to consider. Its Naga range is specifically designed for MMOs, with its most recent model featuring 12 extra buttons on the side. It can be a little unnerving using a mouse with so many extra buttons, but if MMOs are your thing, you'll really appreciate the advantage this can give.

Corsair Vengeance M65

RRP: £67.99
If FPS games are more your thing then you'll definitely want to pick up the Corsair M65. Not only does it have a high 8200 DPI range for great speed and accuracy but it features a toggle-able 'sniper mode', which switches to a low DPI for precision targeting – an important feature for FPS fans. It's quite a heavy mouse too, which is as much a warning as praise – FPS gamers will need that for greater control.

Razer Deathadder

RRP: £74.99
Mostly what makes the Razer Deathadder such a good mouse – and worth its otherwise high price – is in its carefully considered design. This is by far and away one of the best gaming mice in terms of fit, and while it only has two additional buttons for a large majority of games there isn't really much more you need. It's a luxury option but certainly one of the better ones out there.

PART 5 Gaming keyboards

Gaming keyboards are much easier to pinpoint than mice. Where the latter needs to fit a very particular feel, the former is much more objectively measured. The primary choice is between a mechanical keyboard (so the keys are individual switches) and a membrane keyboard. There are pros and cons for both, though mechanical keyboards tend to win out in terms of reliability. Serious gamers should definitely consider a mechanical keyboard, but if you're after a cheaper, more portable option (for LANs perhaps) there are still some great membrane keyboards on the market. Outside of that there isn't really much to distinguish between many options besides their ergonomic design and the extra gadgets they might offer, such as additional, customisable keys.

What to look for

Mechanical versus Membrane – Since this will be your big decision, it's worth spending some time looking at the options. As already mentioned, mechanical keyboards use a system of

separate switches so that each key you press is exactly that – there's no confusion between multiple key presses, they'll last you much longer and they feel more consistent in use. But it does take some getting used to a mechanical keyboard, they are heavier than their membrane counterparts and they are considerably more expensive. Mechanical will always be better in terms of gaming, but it might not be worth the cost.

Cherry MX – If you are looking at mechanical keyboards then you may see the term 'Cherry MX Switches' of varying colours pop up. These are references to the types of mechanical switches being used in that keyboard with red, brown and blue being the most common. Red are unrestricted, linear switches preferred for gaming – their lack of restriction makes them much more responsive. Brown and blue offer a much more tactile response with a noticeable 'bump' to let you know a key has been pressed, with brown being a quieter key and blue still offering the louder click as you type. Your situation will affect which of these you want.

Backlighting – It might seem like a minor thing, but backlighting is quite an important feature to have. It can come in a variety of styles – sometimes just the spaces between the keys, other times just the lettering and sometimes both – and usually the colour and brightness can be customised. It's a good feature to have, especially for LAN attenders – often the dark rooms will make it

hard to see where your fingers are resting, and backlighting will fix that.

Macro/extra keys – Some keyboards bring additional buttons along with them, ranging from a handful of macro keys on the far left to a whole new array often presented like another ten-key number pad. How useful these are will depend on the games you play: MMO and perhaps RTS players will get quite a lot from these extra key binding options, but most players won't really have much use for them. When looking into this feature, try to evaluate how close those extra keys are either to the WASD or the directional buttons, since that will directly correlate to how easy they are to access mid-game.

Media keys – Perhaps less important for gaming, media keys are a set of additional buttons that directly affect any videos or music you might be playing through media software – whether that's skipping or pausing, or increasing and lowering the volume. It's a handy extra to have, admittedly, but be warned that rarely are these buttons hardwired to correspond with the operating systems themselves, meaning you'll likely need to install and run software just to set them up and use them – and even then they're not always reliable.

Wrist rests – Though not entirely a necessary option to include since you can purchase gel wrist rests anyway, it's worth thinking

about the comfort of the keyboard you're going to be buying. If you're spending a lot of money, you'll want to know that it can at least be used in a relaxed manner, and often a rest specialised for the keyboard itself will feel better than an optional gel equivalent. If the keyboard has a longer section (beneath the spacebar) you may not need one anyway, so try to consider the shape of keyboard you're after as well as the position it'll be placed on your desk so you know 100% that it won't cause any damage to your wrists.

Keyboard suggestions

Razer Blackwidow Chroma

RRP: £164.99
This mechanical keyboard offers pretty much everything you might need from a great gaming keyboard: great design, backlighting, a set of customisable keys and non-intrusive software too. While it is expensive, it also comes in three other types down to a non-backlit, number-pad-less model at £79.99.

Corsair K70 Vengeance

RRP: £138.99
Corsair's range ticks all the right boxes with Cherry MX Red

switches, individual backlighting customisation for each key (so you can highlight WASD, for example) and a gripped wrist rest. Alternatives come in the FPS-focus keyboard that comes with contorted movement and weapon select keys, or the K95 – which is essentially the K70 but with a set of 18 bindable keys for MMO players.

Logitech K800

RRP: £99.99
As a better option for LAN events, the wireless Logitech K800 is lightweight and portable while still maintaining a good ergonomic design. It even has backlighting, which could be a benefit in the darkened halls of a LAN. It's all-purpose so not as fancy as the higher-end models, and there's even a wired equivalent if you don't fancy worrying about wireless signals and batteries.

Roccat Arvo Compact

RRP: £59.99
As the name suggests the Arvo Compact is a much smaller keyboard – perfect for carrying around at LANs and slotting in next to another player's rig for some ad-hoc split-screen multiplayer. It is a budget model so doesn't have much in the way of fancy extras, but it is cheap, durable and even features a couple of tweakable macro keys.

PART 5 Monitors

Buying a monitor for gaming is even more arduous than buying a new TV; while you're looking at all the same tech details – such as contrast ratio – you now also want to pay more attention to refresh rate and response time. What this amounts to is a lot of confusing numbers and no real certainty that the one you'll get is the best; hopefully we can dispel some of those concerns. Further questions are derived from how you want your set-up to look: do you want to run multiple screens? A single larger one? A wider screen with an unusual aspect ratio? There are too many options, too many variables to consider, so we've picked out the key facets you need to know about buying the best PC gaming monitor.

What to look for

Aspect ratio – Gaming monitors come in all shapes and sizes, and aspect ratio – or the width of the screen versus the height – is a large reason for this. But as gaming dimensions have become a little more standardised over the years, 16:9 is the standard to aim for. This will be the same as your TV, most likely, and if you're not too fussy about how much of your games you can see then it's easier just to stick with this. If you want a wider viewpoint in-game, however, for a kind of vision more akin to our own human eyes then you might want to look into wider aspect ratios. Again these can be in a variety of sizes, but 21:9 is the more common option, meaning more games are likely to be compatible with this size.

Resolution versus size – It's easy to say 'just go for the highest resolution', but up to a certain point an increase in resolution is actually irrelevant. At around 21 inches you're not really going to need to spend the extra to increase the resolution. If you start going over that, however, you'll probably want to start looking at higher-res screens. This will be affected by the aspect ratio you're going for too, naturally, but with bigger screens you're going to want as high a resolution as possible since it will mean not only more detail in your games but also in every aspect of your PC usage.

Refresh rates and hertz – This is often played up as an important feature for gaming monitors and that's true, it is. However, what many overlook is the possible frame rate you're capable of producing with your games. Your potential frame rate is affected by the graphics card you have installed; if you are only capable of producing 30 frames a second, then it doesn't matter how fast your refresh rate is, it will still be limited by that. If you're capable of 60 or more, however, then you're going to want as fast a refresh rate as possible. 60Hz (or hertz) is the standard for most gaming monitors, but it's not uncommon for 120Hz, 144Hz or 240Hz to be built into modern monitors. If your PC is going to be the best, then you want as high a refresh rate as possible – it'll produce a smoother image, look much nicer during play and will be much more relaxing for your eyes.

Response time – Your monitor's response time is essentially the speed at which it is capable of updating with a new input or image. This is measured in milliseconds, so the lower the better. Most monitors will have a response time of roughly 8ms or less, but the better gaming monitors will measure either 2ms or 5ms. Try not to go for anything worse than 16ms, however, since that's when you'll start noticing a difference.

Type of panels – One last thing to consider is the type of panel you're choosing to use, with choices between the standard TN panels or the newer technology of IPS panels. TN panels are more common and generally offer good brightness and low power consumption, but cheaper monitors can have poor colour accuracy, especially at non-perfect viewing angles. IPS monitors are much better in this regard with practically perfect image clarity at very high viewing angles with great colour reproduction. Sadly they are more expensive as a result, use a lot more power and don't feature the higher refresh rates of TN panels. It's a balancing act, then, but if you're not sparing any expense then an IPS monitor might be the one to go for.

Monitor suggestions

Asus ROG Swift PG278Q

RRP: £619.99
It might be expensive, but it features a 1ms response time, toggle-able refresh rates, NVIDIA's G-Sync technology built in and is even 3D ready. Simply put, it is the best WQHD (Wide Quad HD) monitor out there and if you can afford the expense, it's well worth considering. It might not be a 4k monitor, but at 2560x1440 resolution it's nothing to sneeze at.

Acer XB280HK

RRP: £549.99
While this monitor doesn't have quite the same amount of tech as the Asus ROG Swift, it does have a native 4k screen with the same built-in G-Sync technology. It's cheaper, too, but since it is capable of 4k resolutions it is a monitor that you'll want to pair

up with a pretty powerful rig, otherwise you may find it not quite able to reach all of those pixels – leaving it looking a little fuzzy.

AOC U3477Pqu

RRP: £599.99
If you want a widescreen monitor then AOC – a reputed name in the monitor market – has the one for you. At a resolution of 3440x1440 it edges out over most other widescreen monitors, while its IPS panel means you'll get perfect clarity. The 21:9 aspect ratio might not be ubiquitous with PC gaming just yet, but you'll be glad to try it out for the first time on this screen.

BenQ RL2455HM

RRP: £155.99
You don't want to be lugging expensive screens around to LAN events, so that's where this BenQ monitor comes in. It may only be 1080p, but it sports a 1ms response time, an insanely high contrast ratio of 12 million:1 (meaning deeper blacks and whiter whites) and even built-in speakers (though you'll likely want to be using a headset at LAN events). Recommended for the budget conscious.

PART 5 Headsets

To get the best audio from your PC gaming it might seem counter-intuitive to use a headset, but the personal audio space is a much more immersive experience than even the best PC-compatible stereo systems. Buying a headset isn't quite as littered with jargon as most other accessories, but there are some features you'll want to keep an eye out for. As ever it's about asking the right questions. Do you want the most detailed sound quality? Do you want the clearest microphone and chat options? Do you want something suitable for LANs? It's a minefield of options, but the first step is to know what you're looking for.

What to look for

Ear covering – There are two types of headsets, over-ear and on-ear. The difference might not sound too great, but it basically affects how insulated your sound is. Over-ear headsets have much thicker padding that cover the entirety of the ear; this produces a noise-cancelling effect that means external sounds will be blocked out with varying model-dependent levels of success. While this gives you much better sound while playing, often these headsets can 'pinch' a little – and some users might feel discomfort over extended periods of play, especially with cheaper models. On-ear, conversely, are much lighter and generally sit – as the name suggests – on your ear. External sounds will disrupt your in-game audio, naturally, but the lighter build and fit of these types generally make them more comfortable for longer play.

Microphone types – The quality of any given microphone is dependent on the make and model you're going for, and as always the more you pay the more likely this particular feature will be improved. Noise-cancellation is something you're going to want to look for in a headset microphone, and most will advertise this when it is included. It simply means the microphone will more likely pick up just your voice, rather than other external sounds such as game audio or other people in the same room as you. Look for a directional microphone, i.e. one that points at your mouth, rather than a more typical boom mic, since that's more likely to provide better clarity.

Surround sound – Like with any speaker system, looking for Dolby's surround-sound options is a sure-fire way of spotting a good-quality audio option. This does translate into greater expense, obviously, but when it comes to gaming the added benefit of surround-sound audio can be an important addition. Consider a game like *Call of Duty* or *Battlefield*: being able to detect where an enemy is by listening to the sound of their footsteps or gunfire gives you a much more intuitive, natural advantage that they might not have. So surround sound isn't just about the quality of the audio but the fact that it gives you a step-up in-game. Dolby 7.1 is the best you'll get, but 5.1 and less is viable if you prefer cheaper options.

In-line controls – It seems like such a mundane thing to mention, especially when a large number of headsets all come with controls built into the cable itself. But it's important since these will usually let you alter the volume of both game audio and voice chat via the controls, as well as mute your own microphone. They can come with varying options, so if possible try and take a look at the in-line controls available on any potential purchase so you know your needs are accounted for here.

Frequency response range – Now this might sound like jargon, and to some extent it is, but these days with modern headsets it's largely irrelevant and many don't even bother to advertise the possible range. The frequency response range of any audio device is the measurement of its lowest bass and highest treble, and while the wider the range the better, there is obviously a limit to how much we as humans can hear anyway. Practically every headset these days offers the same range of 20–20,000Hz.

Headset suggestions

Astro A50 7.1

RRP: £270.00
This is easily one of the top-of-the-line models, but for the price you'll get that impressive Dolby 7.1 surround sound, a wireless set (so no fiddling with cables) and an entirely optional but oh-so-appreciated feature that mutes the microphone after being raised away from your mouth. The sound quality you get from this set of cans is very impressive, but considering the price you'd be as well off with any number of cheaper alternatives.

Corsair Vengeance 1500/2100

RRP: £81.98/£86.98
Considering the price, the Corsair Vengeance range has no reason to be as impressive as it is: the build quality is fantastic, the

Dolby 7.1 sound is great and the microphone works a treat. The 2100 is a reasonable upgrade if you fancy a wireless alternative, but there really isn't all that much in it. Just be aware that it is a heavier headset, so could prove a bit weary with extended use. Alternatively, for a cheaper option try Corsair's Raptor range.

Turtle Beach Z300

RRP: £99.99
If all you're after is a decent headset with minimal fuss then the Z300 is the one for you. Though its over-ear form isn't all that good at blocking out external sound, its lightweight wireless design means you can wear it for hours without any worries. It's got a great microphone too, and all you need to connect it to your PC is a USB port for the accompanying dongle – making it a doddle to use at LAN events.

Sennheiser HD 205

RRP: £49.99
As a budget option the Sennheiser HD 205 is a fantastic headset but with a cost: it does not come with a microphone. Multiplayer might not be a hugely important facet of your PC gaming, and in that regard the HD 205 provides a great sound quality to really immerse yourself in. It's a cheap enough alternative for LAN events, too, though again the lack of a microphone might let you down.

 PART

ACCESSORIES

Gaming controllers

With the rising popularity of games consoles it has become increasingly common for their PC equivalents to come with built-in controller functions, often making these games better to play if you discard the keyboard and mouse entirely. Moreover, many recent games – in particular 2D indie games – are often much better when played with a pad in your hand than the claw-shaped hunch you might have traditionally. That might sound incredulous to some hard-core PC gamers, but the truth is that in this day and age having a good-quality gaming controller to hand is imperative for most PC gamers.

What to look for

Games console design – Too often manufacturers try to add to tried-and-tested official console designs, but for no reason. Look for something that tries to keep the simplicity of a console controller (otherwise you're better just sticking with a keyboard), with four face buttons, two analogue sticks, a D-Pad and trigger buttons too. Anything else is an optional extra.

Heavyweight pads – The thing about controllers is, unlike a mouse and keyboard, you're actually holding on to them. It might seem like an odd thing to suggest, but looking for a heavier controller could actually lead to a more comfortable experience; often lightweight controllers have cheaper quality builds, and a heavier weight just feels more compelling to use.

Wired versus wireless – It's a question you might have asked about keyboards and mice, too, but here it's more of a matter of personal taste. A wired controller will give you a much simpler set-up process, while a wireless one obviously gives you greater freedom of movement when playing – even if it does require new batteries or recharging from time to time.

Controller suggestions

Microsoft Xbox 360 controller for PC

RRP: £29.99
This is the very same controller that was so well loved for the Xbox 360 but with a wire. Being a Microsoft product its drivers are built into Windows so in most cases it should be as simple as plugging it into a USB port and playing, without any real struggle. If you already have a wireless Xbox 360 controller, you can even buy a USB adapter and use that.

Razer Sabretooth Elite Gaming Controller

RRP: £79.99
It's much more expensive for what is, essentially, another Xbox 360 controller, but Razer brings a PC mindset to this pad. It's got six sensibly placed, customisable buttons – if that's something you need – an improved D-Pad, backlit 'hyperesponse' face buttons and even the option to tweak the sensitivity of the analogue sticks. It's the option to go for if you really care about a gaming controller.

Sony DualShock 4

RRP: £49.99
Both the latest gaming consoles come with new and improved controllers, and both are compatible with the PC. It's a case of picking your poison, really, but the overall build quality of the DualShock 4 edges it out – even if you will need to download some software to get it to function with your PC. There's not much point getting the Xbox One equivalent if you can pick up a 360 one for less.

Logitech Gamepad F310

RRP: £24.99
If you want to avoid using a controller as much as possible and only want a budget option for when you simply have to use a gamepad, then this will be the one for you. It uses the familiar parallel analogue stick design of the DualShock and is very easy to set up, but it is cheaper and feels it too. A great option to chuck in for the LAN events, however.

PART 5 **Racing wheels**

If racing games are your thing – and there is a great range of simulation racers only on PC – then you really ought to consider the extra expense of a racing wheel, offering an unbeatable experience when monitoring apexes and finding racing lines. You'll need the extra space on your desk to compensate for the size of these things, but if that's not an issue and you're keen to make the most of your virtual driving experience then considering this added extra will add a whole new layer of enjoyment to your racing games.

What to look for

Force feedback – It might not sound like much, but the addition of vibration in a racing wheel is enough to separate a great wheel from an average one. Much like the way console controllers use the vibration to provide extra sensory information for a game, its inclusion in a racing wheel is what helps you distinguish the right points to brake, accelerate and even turn corners. This is a key feature.

Pedals and gear stick – Not every racing wheel will come with a set of pedals and a gearstick, and that might be better for you – the two will take up more room and there is always compensation in the form of on-wheel buttons. But for that true racing experience, for that real sensation that you're in the driver's seat, you should consider at least a set of pedals too.

Rotation angle – This might be low down on the list of important features, but for the authentic experience you're looking for as high a rotation angle as you can possibly get. Many racing wheels lock at a certain angle and while the game will have no problem sensing that as a 'full' turn, most drivers will want as free a steering wheel as possible.

Racing wheel suggestions

Thrustmaster T500RS

RRP: £370.00
Though it is designed for the PS3, the T500RS is compatible with PCs and remains one of the best, sturdiest racing wheels you can buy – though its gearstick is sold separately at around £130. It offers a full 1,080-degree rotation angle, three pedals

(most usually come with just two) and an adjustable pedal panel. This is for devoted enthusiasts only.

Logitech G27

RRP: £299.99
Considered by many to be one of the best racing wheels on the market, the G27 manages to offer the full package for an affordable price. A three-pedal set-up with included gearstick combines with an RPM counter that integrates with your game and extra programmable buttons that really only PC gamers can make the most of.

Logitech Driving Force GT

RRP: £129.99
Again, this wheel is designed for the PS3 (*Gran Turismo* will have that effect) but is compatible with PCs all the same. Only two pedals here but still a fairly robust and complete package all the same. A 900-degree rotation angle still offers a great amount of 'give' in the corners, and it even features adjustment dials to alter traction control and braking bias on the fly.

Thrustmaster Ferrari Racing Wheel Red

RRP: £54.99
As you might expect by the price, Thrustmaster's lower-spec racing wheel is a little more budget quality. It doesn't match the same strength of materials as the higher end of the market and only has a 240-degree rotation angle, but unlike its competitors it features a desk clamp rather than suckers – which means you'll get a great level of stability during use.

PART 5 Joysticks

There's been a resurgence of sorts in flight sims of late, with the likes of *Elite: Dangerous* and *Star Citizen* – among other non-spacefaring equivalents – really ramping up the need for a joystick. Of all the accessories and peripherals available the joystick is perhaps the most antiquated, and as a result the most optional. But much like the effect racing wheels have on driving simulations, a good joystick can have a similar effect on flight simulations. It's certainly a purchase worth considering if you want to get truly suckered into *Elite: Dangerous* et al.

What to look for

Throttle control – This is a distinguishing feature between a good joystick and a bad one, giving you more incremental – and, importantly, tactile – control over your speed, and in the far reaches of space that counts for a lot in dogfights. You're going to want to favour a separate throttle control over something incorporated into the stick itself, but if you're after a budget option you likely won't get that.

Z-axis control – All joysticks will feature X- and Y-axis navigation, meaning left and right, forward and back. For the most part that will be enough, but if you want full control then you'll want to look for Z-axis control, allowing you to twist the joystick clockwise or anti-clockwise to alter your craft's yaw, minimising the number of extra turns you'll need to make to face the right direction.

HOTAS – This stands for 'hands-on throttle and stick', and essentially means that the product you're buying comes with a dual-stick set-up – one for the throttle and one for navigational controls. You'll obviously need to pay more for the extra, but for a more realistic simulation experience having this as a feature will be extremely important.

Number of buttons – With the range of joysticks available on the market, it's easy to go too extreme in this regard. Either you'll have an excessive number of buttons – leading to over-complication and awkward use – or you'll have too few, leaving you reliant on having your keyboard by your side. Think about the game(s) you'd like to play with your joystick, and how many additional buttons you might need.

Joystick suggestions

Saitek X-55 Rhino

RRP: £169.99
While it might not be the most expensive joystick out there, the X-55 has a build quality well worth its admittedly high price, plus twin throttles for control of dual-engine crafts and the addition of the all-important Z-axis control. You can even adjust the springs

controlling the tension of the stick itself, so you can get a pressure that suits your taste.

Thrustmaster HOTAS Warthog

RRP: £369.99
This is perhaps excessively priced and since the set-up doesn't feature Z-axis control it feels like a bit of an unnecessary expense. But it is modelled on the real-world A-10C Thunderbolt II bomber, cased in metallic parts for a robust and realistic feel and features twin throttles and tons of extra buttons (that can be remapped to throttle control). Technically speaking it's not as good as the X-55 Rhino, but it still manages to be well worth the cost for the devoted flight enthusiast.

Thrustmaster T-Flight HOTAS X

RRP: £44.99
As an alternative to the Warthog, Thrustmaster has a great affordable option in the T-Flight HOTAS X set-up. It doesn't feature quite as many bells and whistles as the expensive equivalents, but it does have Z-axis control, which, as we keep saying, is an important feature to include, especially at such a low price.

Logitech Extreme 3D Pro

RRP: £44.99
The Extreme 3D Pro tends to sell for a lot less than its recommended price, making it one of the cheapest joysticks out there. It's also, for the money, one of the better low-end sticks, and though it does have a cheap feel to the buttons it is hard to knock what is an otherwise solid, budget-priced joystick. Perfect for smaller hands, too.

PART 5 Oculus Rift

There's something of a furore over the Oculus Rift. First appearing on crowd-funding site Kickstarter and getting an exceptional response, the gaming community has wholly embraced this new breed of virtual reality. So much so that even Facebook took notice, buying the company outright to ensure it had the right financial backing to see the device truly take off. Facebook's dream, it says, is a world where we don't need to fly around the world to visit old friends, pay over the odds for courtside seat tickets at a big basketball event or even leave the house to host business meetings. It sounds idyllic, but for games – which is what the device is, at the moment, primarily intended for – it offers a whole new level of immersion, and already developers are showcasing what virtual reality can do to drive video games into a whole new space. There are other contenders in the virtual-reality arena – Sony's Project Morpheus, for example, Samsung's Gear VR or even Google Glass – but for the time being the only tangible product you can try is the Oculus Rift.

What you need to know

Still in development – You can buy a virtual-reality Oculus Rift set from its website – and if you're something of a technophile you should be tempted – but it's worth noting that the product that is available now isn't yet the final version. In fact its original model has already been redesigned into an enhanced and improved version, and that's likely to continue until Oculus is happy with the technology it has created. But don't let that put you off: technology is always going to involve an iterative process and even when the final thing is released it will still be regularly updated with newer models – not unlike smartphones and tablets. There's already a handful of games that make use of the Oculus Rift – one of the most popular choices being *Elite: Dangerous* – with many more on the way. There's security in buying a headset now, so if you want to be part of this exciting, burgeoning technology then don't let the fact that it's still early put you off.

Dual-screen view – Rather than a single screen, the Oculus is instead built with two separate, high-resolution screens – one for each eye. This means that you're seeing the game's images the same way that you're seeing real-world images, which means, though it might sound unusual, that your brain interprets these virtual images as it would real images. Combine this with a wide field of view – approximately 100-degrees wide – to better mimic our own real-world field of view and you have a system that truly replicates a human way of seeing virtual worlds.

Dear Esther is a tranquil, exploratory gaming experience more about discovering its story; it is a perfect use of a VR headset

Stereoscopic 3D – While the rest of the world has realised 3D is a bit of a fad, with the Oculus Rift it's actually a key – almost unnoticeable – component of the hardware. To truly make the virtual display work, Oculus Rift features stereoscopic 3D – in both screens, one for each eye – to make objects within the game appear at different distances to you. This provides the necessary sense of depth and scale that you need in a virtual world for it to feel so tangible; it means items closer to you in the game look as though you could actually reach out and touch them, and with some games that's actually possible.

Low-latency head-tracking – One of the biggest problems with virtual reality was always the high latency between your head moving and the camera in the game or VR world moving. It meant the immersion was broken as soon as you started to explore the environment. With advancements in gyroscopic and accelerometer motion control and lighter hardware, the Oculus Rift can better track every subtle movement your head makes, giving you the sensation that you are actually within the virtual room or cockpit.

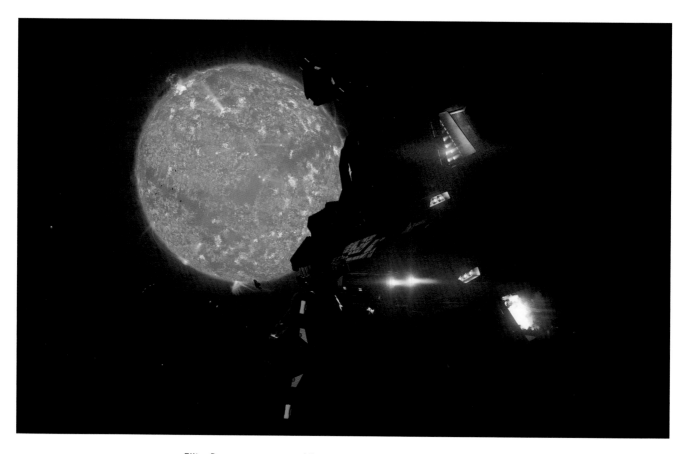

Elite: Dangerous was one of the first games to properly utilise the Oculus Rift headset, and many gamers agree that it really does make for a more involving experience.

Games to try with Oculus Rift

Hawken – Of the games currently working with Oculus Rift, a large portion are set inside cockpits of one form or another. It sort of makes sense – what with the restricted movement – but having you control lumbering mechs is a very cool sensation. Controls-wise it's not too alien to its non-Oculus equivalent, but the fact that the camera is locked inside the mech itself helps make it feel all the more empowering. It helps that *Hawken* is free-to-play, too, so you don't need to pay anything to try it out with the Rift.

Dear Esther – This might not be the most interesting use of Oculus Rift, but the world design of *Dear Esther* is one of the things for which it was so well loved. Though it's only got unofficial support with the Oculus Rift it's easy enough to implement – it seems Valve's Source engine works well with the Rift – but it's worth it just to experience the intricate world of

Dear Esther. It's a more plodding, exploratory game anyway, so the addition of the Oculus Rift makes complete sense.

Elite: Dangerous – Frontier's space-flight simulation is immersive and compelling at the best of times, so the implementation of virtual reality only helps to make it even more fascinating. As you're flying around the deep, dark depths of space you'll be able to peer around your cockpit, and you'll naturally do so. *Elite: Dangerous* has ship details dotted around the cockpit, whether it's engine temperature or incoming notifications. Soon enough you become so engaged by its world while donning a Rift that you'll habitually glance at the necessary details – as you would if you were a real spaceship pilot. This might seem like such a throwaway facet, but it's a truly absorbing way to play – especially when combined with a joystick.

Euro Truck Simulator 2 – This might be one of the more ordinary suggestions on here, but it is all the same a very valid one. *Euro Truck Simulator* offers a very strict, very ordinary set of rules, but somehow through the mundane nature of its gameplay – and the subtle, simulated requirements that are needed of a cargo-transport driver – the game actually becomes stimulating. It's a hard sell, admittedly, but if you like the idea of an unexpected mentally tasking game then you'll certainly want to get this for your Oculus Rift for the ultimate immersive experience.

PART 5 NVIDIA SHIELD

Now you've got the ultimate PC gaming set-up, how about being able to take that on the road with you? For all its benefits, PC gaming is a fairly stationary way of playing – unless you have a console for your PC. That's what the NVIDIA SHIELD can do, and its variety of options means you can pick and choose how you want to play. There's a controller with a built-in screen, or you can get a tablet and controller combo for a bigger screen to enjoy your games on. Truth be told, you don't actually need a gaming PC to play any games on it – a Netflix-like streaming service, NVIDIA's GRID, means you can stream high-end PC games to the device. Or you can buy Android games and play them on the go. But best of all is how you can stream your own gaming collection wirelessly, meaning you can play on your PC and continue where you left off when you're not home or just relaxing in the living room. It's a great little gadget that comes with a heap of benefits.

What you need to know

The right choice – You have two options here: the cheaper NVIDIA SHIELD Portable Console, or the tablet and controller combo. The portable console combines a controller with a small screen and, though it's not the most ergonomic device, its compact, portable, all-in-one design makes a great companion for those who travel a lot. The alternative is more expensive and comes with two separate parts: an Android tablet and a controller. This is a bigger screen and allows for four controllers to be synced at once. It is still portable, of course, but the separate parts means it's better suited to home use.

Built on Android – The tablet and portable console are both built on Android, meaning the open operating system will allow you to handle many of the same things Android smartphones and tablets can do. The fact that it comes with access to the Google

Play store – and that many Android games feature controller support – means that you'll have access to a wide range of gaming options, even beyond your own list of PC games.

PC streaming – Honestly, GameStream is the big selling point for the NVIDIA SHIELD, letting you stream your games from the PC to whichever handheld device you've settled on. It's a built-in feature and works over Wi-Fi and, as long as you have a steady and fast enough Internet connection, you should have no problems accessing this feature. You will need an NVIDIA GPU – for access to the NVIDIA GeForce Experience software – but if you do, you'll have no problems setting it up; it really is just a case of enabling an option in the settings. Do be aware that not every game is compatible with GameStream, but most major games do include controller support, which is a good sign of what will work. You can find a full list online at **http://shield. nvidia.com/pc-game-list/**

NVIDIA GRID – An alternative to GameStream, GRID is more akin to Netflix by letting you access a number of games you don't own by streaming them from a supercomputer in the cloud. It's definitely worth checking out if you can. The list of available games isn't exactly vast, but new games are added every Tuesday so you can be sure that there's always something new to play. It's a great addition for anyone who travels a lot.

PART 6 Overclocking your gaming PC

Overclocking is a bit of a scary-sounding phrase. To those who don't know the rules of engagement it just sounds dangerous. Those who do know of overclocking, but have never done it, are likely put off by the stories and they've heard the seriousness with which the phrase is often used. Overclocking is seen as the reserve of elite PC enthusiasts, but in truth it's not too difficult to do – and when done properly it's not nearly as risky as you might imagine.

Overclocking lets you access more power from your processor, graphics card and even memory by overriding their factory settings and tinkering with them to best optimise them for your own PC hardware and set-up. It can mean squeezing the very best performance out of your system, or enhancing older parts so that they last a little bit longer. Understanding overclocking means you can make the most out of your gaming PC, and it's a helpful way of saving on upgrades or the initial budget.

Since overclocking does mean you're tampering with the base optimal settings, it will mean those parts will run hotter, and higher temperatures can lead to failing hardware – and not only the parts that you've overclocked. Yet remember that these factory settings are often set quite a bit lower than they need to be, making the out-of-the-box hardware you buy for your PC more likely to be compatible with a wide range of PCs and suffer fewer faults as a result. In the eyes of the manufacturer it's better to be safe than sorry, so don't let the potential issues put you off. That's not to say you shouldn't be careful, of course: it's a gradual process of incremental upgrades, and if you are interested in attempting to supercharge your PC then you need to do so in small stages with regular tests. In that sense it can be a bit of a laborious task, but much like the thrill of putting together your first gaming PC the sensation of reaching new and better benchmarking tests can be enough of a thrill to get enthusiasts interested.

To help you get your head around overclocking your hardware we've detailed everything you need to know to assist in your own overclocking adventures. Since every piece of hardware is different, there's no sure-fire, step-by-step method to unlocking your PC's full potential, but as long as you have the knowledge to follow the process without any concern then you'll soon find it's not nearly as scary as it first sounds. We'll also document some of the best, most useful pieces of software you'll need for benchmarking – the process of stress-testing your PC to ensure your changes are safe – and some of the most popular games and applications overclockers like to use to show off just how powerful their PCs really are.

Every BIOS will look different, from older blue screen styles like this to more modern, higher resolution options – often with black screens.

```
      CMOS Setup Utility - Copyright (C) 1984-2011 Award Software

   ▶ MB Intelligent Tweaker(M.I.T.)        Load Fail-Safe Defaults

   ▶ Standard CMOS Features                Load Optimized Defaults

   ▶ Advanced BIOS Features                Set Supervisor Password

   ▶ Integrated Peripherals                Set User Password

   ▶ Power Management Setup                Save & Exit Setup

   ▶ PC Health Status                      Exit Without Saving


   Esc : Quit                   ↑↓→←: Select Item      F11 : Save CMOS to BIOS
   F8  : Q-Flash                F10 : Save & Exit Setup  F12 : Load CMOS from BIOS

              Change CPU's Clock & Voltage
```

PART

Understanding overclocking

Before you actually jump into the overclocking itself, it is important that you first understand the technical side of what it is you're trying to achieve. Every piece of hardware is different; one part could be minutely different to another of the exact same make and model due to the manufacturing process, so it's important to know what you're changing and what effect that change has. To help we'll going to explain some of the terms you'll need to understand when overclocking – that way you won't have any problems when overclocking your own system. And since you can enhance the performance of parts such as your graphics card, processor and memory, we'll try to keep this section as general as possible across all forms of overclocking.

Key terms to learn

Overclocking – Let's start with the phrase itself, which is fairly self-explanatory. Overclocking is the process of increasing the clock speed of a particular piece of PC hardware to run faster than its initial factory settings, unlocking performance gains. Additionally this can mean increasing the voltage that piece of hardware accepts to help it attain higher speeds.

BIOS – This is the set-up screen where you'll do your adjustments to the hardware – the actual process of overclocking itself. This is essentially the software hardwired into your motherboard, and lets you control the system's hardware and how it performs. You may have seen the BIOS before or you may not have needed to, but either way it is always accessed immediately after starting the system up.

Clock – With all this mention of 'clocks' you're probably asking 'What is a clock?' Well, this is the microchip inside your computer that regulates timing, that vibrates when electricity is applied. It is measured in hertz, with a 2.0GHz processor capable of two billion cycles – or vibrations – a second. It is often represented in your BIOS as 'BCLK'. This is your base clock speed, and is used to calculate your CPU's overall speed: so if your system has a base clock of 100MHz (perhaps shown as slightly under that) with a CPU multiplier or ratio of 30 then your CPU will have a total speed of 3,000MHz, or 3.0GHz. Increasing the multiplier to 33 will make your CPU a 3.3GHz processor.

Data buses – There are multiple buses inside your computer, but the most important is the main one connecting your CPU to the rest

If you want to achieve the very best graphics from your games, overclocking can be a good option for achieving that with cheaper or mid-range parts.

of the system. It is the communication interface that transfers data from your processor to the rest of your PC's hardware, so essentially its speed affects how fast the other parts of your computer can be given commands from the CPU. These can come in various forms, but the function is always the same. Older processors call this the frontside bus (or FSB), while more recent terms include AMD's EV6 or Intel's QuickPath Interconnect. Though these don't all work in exactly the same way, they do control the processing of information and so are pivotal to understand when overclocking.

Clock multiplier/ratio – Otherwise known as CPU multiplier, bus/ core ratio or internal multiplayer, this is the number of times the processor's own internal clock completes a cycle within every external clock count. This is used to calculate the total speed of your processor by multiplying the clock multiplier with the external clock's speed. It is one of the first numbers you'll want to try and adjust in the overclocking process.

Voltage – This is an extra side to overclocking that is important to understand. While increasing the voltage supply to a particular piece of hardware won't actually increase its performance – much like putting extra fuel into a car – it is often a necessity as you increase the speed of that component. The faster an overclocked part runs the more power it's going to need to function at its best. As with the overclocking process, this should be done slowly and incrementally, to ensure the right voltage is set.

Benchmarking – This is a process whereby you will monitor your PC – often under stress-test situations – to ensure that the upgrade you have made to a piece of hardware has both been successful and isn't likely to cause any damage to your hardware. Even outside of overclocking, benchmarking is a useful way of discovering just how powerful your PC is. Since there is a risk of permanent damage to your components by overclocking, it's imperative that you use benchmarking to ensure you haven't exceeded any boundaries. We'll talk in more depth about benchmarking and the software you can use later in this chapter.

DirectX – When it comes to graphics cards, you'll often see the term DirectX pop up – often seen as DX9 or DX11. This is an API that a lot of modern games rely on to function, and though it's not a prerequisite for PC gaming a large portion of games do need a compatible graphics card to function well. Thankfully your only concern is whether or not you're running a DX9 or a DX11 card. DX11 is a more recent, up-to-date and powerful version of DirectX, and enables a lot of fancy extras within games, and most recent GPUs are powerful enough to handle DX11. Make sure you know which yours is, however, before going about overclocking, as it'll help you understand which games you're best testing it with.

Preparation

Before you actually start overclocking there are a few things you'll want to consider first. This will mean downloading and installing some software to help monitor your changes – and stress-test those that you have made – as well as consider some of the hardware requirements for overclocking. This latter part might not be relevant to you, but it's worth knowing about if it is something you want to do in the future.

CPU-Z and GPU-Z help you to monitor your system's processor and graphics card respectively to ensure that your overclocking changes are functioning.

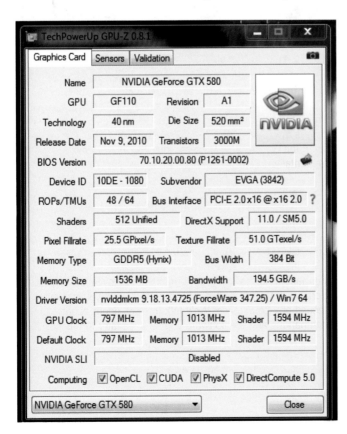

CPU-Z/GPU-Z – This is a very handy piece of software that details your system's various values, such as clock speed, voltage and so on. It's good to run prior to any changes you make and then again after to first ensure that the changes have been maintained properly but also to check that the settings you've altered are working correctly. The equivalent software for when you come to overclock your graphics card is called GPU-Z.

Stress-test software – There's a wide variety of stress-test software available, and it differs with the type of hardware you're overclocking. We'll talk about them in closer detail in each specific section, but for CPU stress-testing you're looking for the likes of Prime95, BurnInTest, FurMark or AIDA64. There are plenty more you can use, but if you're concerned then by all means use a combination of different stress-test software – we can't emphasise enough the importance of making sure your changes won't damage your hardware. For GPU overclocking it's a little simpler, but the easiest to recommend is FutureMark's 3DMark.

Real Temp – Since there's a point to all this stress-testing, you're going to need software to run alongside it. Real Temp will let you monitor the true temperature of all your hardware components to ensure that they aren't overheating during the stress test.

Cooling – If all you're doing is making small upgrades through overclocking then you might not need to worry too much about cooling. As long as your system has enough ventilation and a cooling system suitable for the hardware you have, then smaller changes to the hardware will likely pass without having to change your cooling. In fact, the stock CPU fan should be enough to slightly bump up your processor's power. That's not to say you shouldn't keep an eye on the heat of your system, because that's the biggest threat when overclocking. If you want to make bigger changes then you'll definitely need to make sure that the higher temperature of your computer and its parts are being rectified.

Power supply – It's highly unlikely that you'll need to upgrade your power supply, but since you will be increasing the voltage your parts are using during the overclocking process then the overall power your machine will need will increase too. Chances are you'll have a PSU installed that more than adequately supplies your machine, but if you've got a lower supply of power and find your machine isn't running sufficiently after the overclocking process, it could be that you'll need to upgrade the PSU.

Overclocking compatibility – Not all motherboards, or indeed processors and graphics cards, are suitable for overclocking. Some manufacturers prefer to keep things locked down, while others unlock the potential of their hardware for enthusiasts by default. Thankfully, most high-end PC gaming components are built with overclocking in mind, though you do tend to pay a premium for them.

PART 6

Overclocking your CPU

CPU overclocking is the most common form of enhancement, but when it comes to gaming you might actually want to overclock your graphics card instead since it handles a large portion of how the game actually looks. The CPU handles computational commands, however, so if you want to improve the speed with which processing is handled then it's the CPU you want to upgrade. It's worth remembering that not all hardware is the same, and that even the exact same components could differ in terms of theoretical maximum – even experienced overclockers need to follow the incremental process. Certain makes and models of hardware are better suited towards overclocking, too, though these days modern parts are a little more open in that regard.

When overclocking your processor you're going to be spending a large portion of time in your BIOS. It looks intimidating, so have a poke around – you can always exit without making changes.

With so many variants in hardware, it's impossible to give a definitive step-by-step process when it comes to overclocking. However, the changes you make are generally the same; just remember to be careful, methodical and incremental about the changes you do make. And always stress-test each subtle change.

1. Test the machine
First things first: you're going to want to know what your machine is capable of unchanged. This will give you a solid base for knowing how your machine should be running once you've changed the settings. Using the software suggested previously, such as Prime95 alongside CPU-Z and Real Temp, stress-test the machine. Make a note of the figures you're reaching, both unstressed and stressed. It might seem unimportant, but this will help you to know whether an overclocked part is functioning well.

2. Access the BIOS
After you've got the details for the machine in its default state, you'll want to start the process of overclocking. Reboot your system and, as it starts up, press the correct key to initiate the BIOS screen. This differs between motherboards, often requiring you to press the 'delete' key when prompted or one of the 12 function keys at the top of the keyboard. A screen with the motherboard's manufacturer's name will appear, and it is often here that you'll be told which button to press to load the BIOS system set-up screen. Failing that, take a look inside your motherboard's manual – it'll tell you in there.

3. Find the CPU frequency settings
What you're looking for is the list of settings that control how the CPU functions. Again this differs between processors and motherboards, so you'll need to search around the BIOS for these settings. Look for CPU frequencies, BCLK or base clock speeds, multipliers and ratios or some of the other terms detailed in the 'Key terms to learn' section. You can also refer to your motherboard manual to find the section you need when overclocking. At this point don't change anything, just take note of some of the default settings and confirm you're looking at the right screen.

4. Adjust the CPU settings
Once you're feeling confident, you can begin by adjusting the settings of the CPU. This should be a very incremental process. While it's good to search online for some example settings other users have achieved through overclocking – and in this regard you should always take an average, rather than a maximum – to give you a good idea of what you might be able to reach, remember that all parts are different. Even if you're certain of the numbers you'll be able to reach, you should still go through the process gradually to ensure that your hardware is overclocked safely.

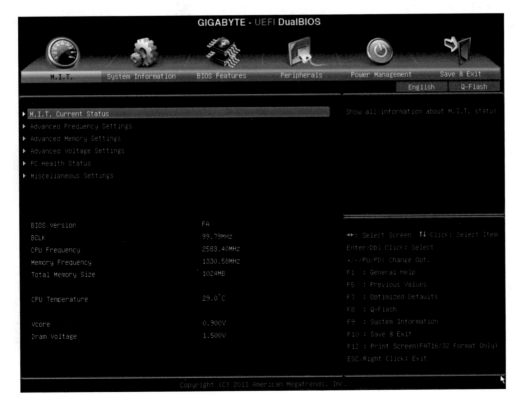

Where your particular motherboard stores the CPU frequency settings differs from board to board. Some will bundle it all in one screen, others within separate menus.

When it comes to multi-core processors, you may be able to unlock the ability to customise the frequency of your CPU depending on how many of the cores are active.

5. Increase the multiplier

You should start by changing your CPU's multiplier – though this might actually be termed clock ratio in your BIOS. This base setting could be anywhere between 15 and 35, depending on the base clock speed (BCLK) of your system. By increasing the multiplier/ratio, you're effectively increasing the number of cycles the processor completes each second. It might be tempting to simply select the highest number, but don't – this would likely be disastrous for your CPU. Instead increase the number by only one or two points. As we've said, it is safer to make these changes slowly, testing all the while. Additionally it's worth noting that some set-ups will allow you to specify individual multipliers depending on how many CPU cores are in use – Intel calls this Turbo Boost mode. If you prefer to tailor your system that way, you'll need to enable the mode and specify individual multipliers for when one, two, three and four of the CPU's cores are active, scaling downwards to allow for optimum use. After the changes save the settings and restart the system, booting into Windows. If your system is locked and not well suited to overclocking then you may not be able to adjust the multiplier, and in that case you'll need to adjust the base clock speed instead, but we'll talk about that soon. It's much better to change a single setting each time rather than make multiple BIOS changes at once – this will help you diagnose a problem if your system throws faults after the changes. It's handy to write down the different changes you make, allowing you to better keep track of the numbers and readjust to a previous functioning setting in case of faults.

6. Stress test

After making a change in the BIOS and rebooting you then need to ensure the settings have stuck and that they are safe for your system. To begin with keep an eye on the system start-up for

anything unusual: any errors will give you a sure sign the change caused a problem, as will forced reboots, but is the system taking especially long to start up? It shouldn't and this might be a sign that there is a problem. Once at the Windows screen, boot up CPU-Z to ensure that the changed settings have been made, then start up your choice of stress-test software. Remember that gaming is one of the most taxing functions a PC can do – at least 3D games – so it might in fact be better to run a combination of stress-test software to make sure your system is safe at full load. Pairing up the likes of BurnInTest and FurMark is a good, and fairly quick, way of ensuring your CPU and GPU can handle the increase in power. Remember to run Real Temp too to ensure that your system isn't reaching dangerous temperatures. Even with this stress-test software, you might want to consider running a high-end, graphically intensive game (we have some examples later in the chapter) to ensure that the upgrade is safe. If the game locks up, freezes, stutters, crashes or you find your system getting far too hot then you'll know something needs to be done.

7. In case of faults

If there is any kind of fault during this process then before repeating the stage again you'll need to find the reason for this fault and rectify it. The faults you come across could include forced restarts or shutdowns, failed stress-tests, unexpected error messages during start-up or failing or erratic running of games. This is likely caused by one of two things: either your increased strain is causing the processor to overheat, thus forcing your PC to shut down as a failsafe measure or it could be that the processor is not getting enough power to run the adjustment. It's likely that early on in the overclocking process the lack of power will be the problem, in which case you'll need to adjust the voltage going to your processor (next step). It could make sense to readjust the change you made to its previous figure to make sure that the fault was caused by this change; if it still occurs at this point, there may be a bigger problem with your PC or individual components.

8. Increase the voltage

With a small change it's unlikely that you'll need to increase the voltage supply, but if your stress-testing does raise problems then it's likely that the upgraded CPU isn't getting enough power to let the improvement function. To do this you'll need to once again head into your BIOS and look for the voltage settings, often referred to as 'Vcore' and usually in a different menu. As with before it will differ depending on your motherboard, but there will be a setting for CPU/Core voltage somewhere in there. You don't need to adjust the voltage settings by much at a time, and again it should always be a gradual upgrade – more voltage going into the component will increase its running temperature so you want to be very conservative with your changes. A voltage increase of 0.0500 at a time is often enough, but remember to keep an eye on the CPU temperature after each tweak you make. As before, save the voltage change and stress-test the machine again.

9. Repeat the process

This is the easiest way of overclocking your CPU, and providing your parts are open to overclocking you should have no problems following it from here. Repeat the process of slowly increasing the multiplier/clock ratio and the core voltage, stress-testing as you go until you have a setting you're happy with. As you increase the voltage remember to keep an eye on the running temperature of your CPU. A maximum of 85°C is generally considered safe, but always search online for the right temperature for your processor. And remember that the higher the temperature and the harder you run your components the more likely you are to decrease their lifespan – like anything that gets excessive use, really. It's not always better to overclock your machine until it is needed for this reason.

10. Increasing the clock speed

If you've got locked components then you won't be able to adjust the multiplier/clock ratio through the BIOS, but that doesn't mean you can't still overclock. You may still be able to subtly increase the base clock to maximise your potential gains. This can cause a greater strain on your system as a whole, especially as adjusting the base clock can also have a knock-on effect with other components – such as the various data buses transferring information between each part – and these may not work well with increased speeds, so exercise a lot of caution when making these changes. To adjust the clock speed you need to once again enter the BIOS and look for the CPU frequencies menu – most likely in the same menu or submenu where you found the multiplier/clock ratio options. Look for the reference to your base clock speed: in Intel chips you're probably looking for 'BCLK', but in AMD chips you may be adjusting the data bus instead, so look for 'FSB' or something similar. Your motherboard manual will have all the details you need. As with the multiplier you want to slowly increase the speed at which the base clock speed performs (measured in MHz), save the settings and then reboot the system into Windows to stress-test. The increments by which it can be increased won't be too vast, and that's for the best – as always, slow and steady is preferred here.

11. Move on to GPU or RAM

Once you've settled on a speed and running standard for your CPU, you may be hungry to adjust even more of your PC. Remember that you can always enable multi-core overclocking on some quad-core chips, and that will give you even greater control – especially when it comes to games, since rarely are all four cores of a chip used in computation for games. After that you'll likely want to overclock your graphics card, which will, in most cases, be bearing the brunt of your PC's computation when it comes to games. Even your RAM can be overclocked, enabling it to run at the speed it is intended to, since most memory is actually underclocked initially.

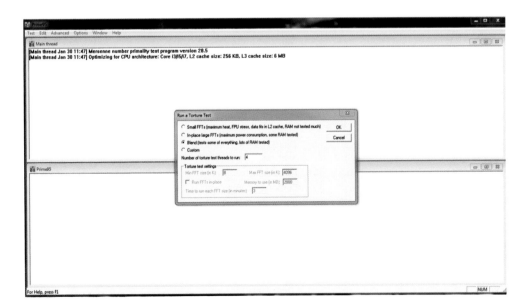

There's a wide range of stress-testing software available. Prime95 shown here is good for overall system tests, great for overclocking your CPU or RAM.

PART  Overclocking your graphics card

While overclocking your processor is certain to help your PC handle more demanding tasks and is one of the first things you'll think of when overclocking your PC, the graphics card should perhaps be the first target of overclocking for PC gamers. These days the GPU is the piece of hardware that handles the bulk of processing when it comes to 3D gaming, so if you want to make your games look as good or play as smoothly as possible – especially if you've gone for a cheaper option to save overall costs on your build – then you'll want to follow these steps. Thankfully it's a little easier to do than with a CPU, though the elements you'll be changing are largely the same. It can be handled in Windows through dedicated GPU overclocking software, so it's much less arduous when changing different factors. As with CPU overclocking, however, every GPU is different, even between otherwise identical makes and models, so you should make small changes at a time, testing them with benchmarking software as you do.

1. Install the drivers

Most GPU software these days will prompt you when a new, non-beta, version of your graphics card's drivers are available, but even if they don't then it's often better to install the latest drivers before you start overclocking your GPU. You'll find these on either the manufacturer's website or the brand's website, allowing you to download and install the most recent software available. In some cases you may be able to download beta drivers as soon as they're available, which is something some gamers do to get the absolute most out of their GPUs – when it comes to overclocking, however, avoid doing this since these beta drivers can sometimes be unstable. Having the most recent, non-beta drivers will give your GPU the absolute best compatibility with your own system and the games you will play.

2. Benchmark your GPU

As with CPU overclocking, you want to start by finding out what your graphics card is capable of. There is a lot of potential benchmarking software to use so we've dedicated a section to it;

It's always good to keep your drivers up to date, especially if you want to get the most from recent games. It's imperative you do it before overclocking, however.

if you don't know which software to use, take a look at that to get a better idea of what you might want to download. As with stress-testing, this will push your graphics card to the maximum, testing its ability to render models, calculate lighting and even its control of physics. Different benchmarking software works in different ways, but the result is the same – to find out how well your GPU performs. Run the benchmarking software and take a note of your GPU's default performance.

3. Run MSI Afterburner
Since GPU overclocking can be done with Windows software there are, as you might expect, a large number of options open to you. For the sake of ease, however, we're going to suggest using MSI Afterburner, which is easy to use and provides a uniform experience for most graphics cards. You're welcome to find and download your own preferred option, but this is the most robust and most widely used option available. AMD cards come with Catalyst Control Center, which enables a similar set of functions if you prefer a safer option, however MSI Afterburner also allows control over the voltage of your card for maximum overclocking potential.

4. Adjust the clock speed
Look for the clock speed setting in MSI Afterburner. It'll be a slider bar with 'min' on one end and 'max' on the other. As ever you want to avoid sliding it up to the maximum, since that could just overload your card and potentially cause damage. Firstly, if there is also a Shader Clock speed then you want to link this to the Core Clock speed too, which is done with the button on the right-hand side in MSI Afterburner. You'll want to adjust the two simultaneously for the best results. Just increase the clock speed by a small amount – 10MHz at a time is enough – then apply the changed setting ahead of benchmarking. If you're

using MSI Afterburner you'll want to save these settings to one of the software's profiles, a function that lets you toggle between overclocked changes – a great option if you want to protect your GPU's lifespan.

5. Benchmark the changes
Now you'll want to test the changes you've made, but first boot up GPU-Z to ensure that the changes to the settings have successfully been applied. Once you've confirmed the changes, run your benchmark software of choice to find out how it compares with your previous test, all the while keeping an eye on the temperature of your graphics card. If you have a high-end GPU then you shouldn't encounter many problems during the benchmark after your first overclocking change. If you have a medium- or low-end card then you may notice some frame-rate issues (most benchmarking software ramps up the demand later on in the test), but so long as the test completes successfully, doesn't get too hot and provides you with a clear improvement then you can consider the change a success.

6. Repeat the clock speed increase
If your benchmarking was a success then you can repeat the process of increasing your GPU's clock speed at 10MHz at a time. It's good to research your particular graphics card to find out what sort of figures most people have achieved to give you a good idea of what you can aim for, but don't let that tempt you into pushing up the numbers quickly; to reiterate, every card is different and yours might not achieve the same overclocking changes as another. Keep gradually increasing the clock speed until your benchmarking causes a problem: your graphics card driver might crash, the screen might go black or graphical artefacts might appear during the benchmarking. Additionally

It's important to test each change you make to ensure it has both been a success and won't damage your graphics card in the process.

your card may be reaching intolerable temperatures, which will cause permanent damage if left in that state. At this point you've gone past the current maximum for your GPU and you should reduce it back down to the last successful clock speed.

7. Increase the voltage

If you're using MSI Afterburner or other software that allows the adjustment of voltage to your GPU then at this point you can try and further your graphics card's capabilities. Be aware that increasing the voltage to your GPU will increase the temperature it runs at, as well as put the card under greater duress – meaning its lifespan could be decreased. Though it will allow you to reach greater clock speeds, if you're not willing to risk your graphics card in this way, you can skip this step. To adjust the voltage of your GPU you'll first need to unlock the feature. In MSI Afterburner that means going into the settings and looking for the 'Unlock Voltage Control' option. Once done you can then adjust the voltage as you did with the core clock; each card controls voltage at its own increments, so type in an increase of 10mV and the software will automatically scale it to the right amount. With this extra power you can now try and readjust the clock speed as you did in step six, gradually increasing it by 10MHz each time and running your benchmark software to ensure the change has been safe. Once you begin to see problems in the benchmarking process again, increase the voltage by another 10mV and repeat the process. When increasing your voltage make sure you know what the safe maximum voltage of your graphics card is, as you absolutely do not want to exceed that. Additionally you need to pay extra attention to the temperature increasing – 80°C is considered safe, while 90°C is generally considered excessive, but remember to search online for the safe maximum temperature for your card.

8. Increase the memory clock speed
Once you've found a safe overclock that you're happy with, you can then repeat the process for the GPU's memory clock speed. This is the exact same process as the GPU clock-speed increase, except you're altering the memory clock-speed slider instead. As before a process of gradual alterations, GPU-Z checks and benchmark tests will be important to find the perfect maximum. It's perhaps safer to take a note of your new GPU clock speed and voltage settings and reset them to the defaults before changing the GPU memory clock speed. Then, if all goes well, use the new settings for GPU clock speed, voltage and GPU memory clock speed to see how it all works together. As always only change one setting at a time so you can easily resolve a problem should you encounter one. You're not going to notice quite as many gains from increasing the memory clock speed, but it's still beneficial in order to get the most out of your GPU.

9. Test it out
Once you've found overclocked settings that you're happy with, and benchmarking tells you they are safe, the important thing to do is to test it all out. Boot up some graphically intensive games to ensure that your settings are safe in a 'real' situation. While benchmarking is great for finding the potential maximum, the added dynamism of gaming can often cause greater stress that the predictability of benchmarking software fails to replicate. If you ever get any issues with your graphics card while playing games – such as regular GPU drivers crashing or black screens – then you should readjust your overclocked settings a little, lowering them and retesting to ensure everything is safe for your GPU. And, as always, keep an eye on those temperatures.

You can use any other software that enables GPU overclocking functionality, but MSI Afterburner is particularly easy to use for practically any make and model of graphics card.

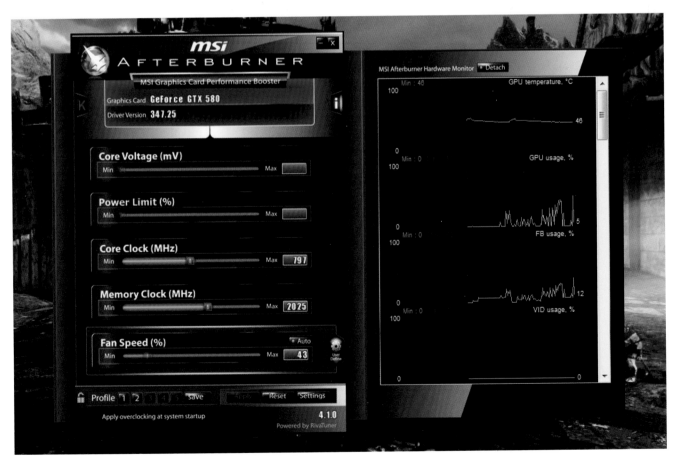

PART 6 Overclocking your memory

With so many different types and grades of RAM, and even varying sizes and capabilities within each type, it can be something of a minefield trying to navigate the complications of overclocking your system's memory. Add in the fact that some parts are considerably better suited to overclocking than others and the fact that the performance gains are comparatively small, and it can seem a somewhat fruitless task. All the same, if you are looking to squeeze every last ounce out of your PC then you may feel you want to manually reconfigure your RAM settings to get your money's worth. But because of all these varying factors, it's not suitable for a step-by-step guide to overclocking your RAM; instead we'll presume you have at least tweaked your CPU settings (since you'll want to do that first anyway), so you've already experienced your system's BIOS. Here then we're going to detail some of the things you need to look out for when overclocking your memory, and explain how you can go about doing it.

Key things to know

Testing software – As with any form of overclocking, it's always good to test the changes you've made. When it comes to RAM it's a little trickier to test, of course, but there is software that can help. First you'll want to make use of CPU-Z, as you have with overclocking the processor, while Prime95 is a good overall system stress-tester. Specifically for RAM, though, you can download testing software such as MaxMem or SiSoftware's Sandra, which will check the memory for its new potential.

Frequency – Most commonly referred to as the DRAM frequency, this is the speed at which your RAM is capable of running. It'll say the speed your memory will be able to run at on the packaging, in the RAM's product description, or even printed on the label on the RAM itself. It is measured in MHz from very low-end at 333MHz to 2,400MHz and over. It's a large part of what affects how quickly your RAM can send and receive data. You'll find this option in your BIOS and it can be adjusted to better match what your RAM is expected to achieve, but remember

CPU-Z also lets you monitor the current settings of your memory, so try to use it after every change you make to your memory to check that the changes have been made successfully.

all hardware is different – even if you have increased your RAM frequency to the number it says on the label, you may still encounter problems and will have to lower it slightly. As ever, the faster it will run the more strain you'll be putting it under, so it's better to find your maximum RAM frequency and drop it down a single setting to maintain reliable regular use from your memory. Also remember that your memory will be limited by what your FSB is capable of – and as we discussed in the CPU section, that can often be changed manually. If you want to know more, read the next point.

FSB:DRAM – In CPU-Z you'll see this figure, which is the FSB to DRAM frequency ratio. Associated with the point on frequency above, it tells you how fast one part is running with regard to the other. Your RAM will always be limited by the speed of your FSB, so you want to try and have that ratio as close to 1:1 as possible – if the FSB is faster than your memory then you're going to get a bottleneck, and the speed of your RAM will limit the FSB. Alternatively it is not necessarily worse to have the RAM running faster than the FSB, because while the latter will bottleneck the former the way your memory accesses data (and its purpose in a computer system anyway) will mean it being faster is not really a negative. Where possible try to make sure your FSB:DRAM ratio is either 1:1 or has the larger number on the right-hand side.

RAM timings – The second most important number for your memory is its set of timings, often advertised as 'CAS' (Column Address Strobe) or 'CAS Latency' even though the latter is technically inaccurate. There are a variety of different timings,

| Memory Timing Mode | Auto |
| Memory Boot Mode | Auto |

▼ Channel A Standard Timing Control

CAS Latency	Auto
tRCD	Auto
tRP	Auto
tRAS	Auto

▼ Channel A Advanced Timing Control

tRRD	Auto
tWTR	Auto
tWR	Auto
tWTP	Auto
tWL	Auto
tRFC	Auto
tRTP	Auto
tFAW	Auto
Command Rate (tCMD)	Auto

Auto = Automatically configures memory sub-timings.
Manual = Manually configure memory sub timings with settings applied to both channels simultaneously.
Advanced Manual = Manually configure both memory channels individually.

↔: Select Screen ↑↓/Click: Select Item
Enter/Dbl Click: Select
+/-/PU/PD: Change Opt.
F2 : Smart Tweak Mode
F5 : Previous Values
F7 : Optimized Defaults
F8 : Q-Flash
F9 : System Information
F10 : Save & Exit
F12 : Print Screen(FAT16/32 Format Only)
ESC/Right Click: Exit

Copyright (C) 2014 American Megatrends, Inc.

The four timing figures you need to change for overclocking your RAM are CAS Latency, tRCD, tRP and tRAS. That's the order they will appear in, too.

but there are four key figures to look out for. These can be found on the label on the RAM itself, and are usually styled with four different digits separated by a dash, for example: 13-15-15-28. These timings represent the various delays that your RAM will be put under when handling data, so the lower the number the better. While it might be advertised at these timings, it might be capable of much shorter delays. Using CPU-Z and the RAM timings given earlier as a guide, the four figures you're looking to change are:

CAS Latency (CL), in this case 13
RAS# to CAS# Delay (tRCD), in this case the first 15
RAS# Precharge (tRP), in this case the second 15
Cycle Time (tRAS), in this case 28

Lowering RAM timings – While we could explain what these timings do and what they affect, that in itself is not too important; instead we'll explain how to proceed to lower the timings. In the BIOS you want to look for the DRAM timing configuration, looking for the four different timings referenced in the point

above. As always this should be a staged process as you discover the lowest delay you can apply to these settings, changing one setting at a time, saving and then testing your change once back in Windows. You can use the base timings as a guide for what kind of ratio each timing can be lowered to – so in our example the CL of 13 would end up at a lower number than the tRCD and tRP. The Cycle Time (or tRAS) will always be higher than the rest. There's a lot more manipulation involved with memory overclocking than the likes of CPU or GPU overclocking, so be prepared for a lot of system restarts. If your PC fails to boot then the last setting you changed was too low.

Command Rate (CR) – You'll basically get two numbers for this, either 1T or 2T. 1T is always faster than 2T, but the increase in performance is marginal at best, so you may not feel the need to change it since running it at 2T is more stable. If you are looking to maximise every aspect of your PC, however, and providing your memory is capable of running 1T, then this can be a quick and easy change to make. You'll find the option in your BIOS with the rest of the memory options.

Voltage – As with all hardware, increasing the voltage will allow you to increase the frequency, or speed, at which it runs. And, as with all hardware, it's important to remember that increasing the voltage will also increase the risk of damage to the component. The risk is greater for RAM, however, since there is no innate fail-safe to protect the component from damage, such as forced shut-offs like with your CPU and GPU. This means you have to be especially careful if you want to increase the voltage of your RAM; find out what the 'right' setting for your memory is, as well as what its absolute maximum is. If you want to be careful then use very conservative voltage increases if at all.

SPD – Serial Presence Detect is a way for manufacturers to supply a set of viable changes to the memory. These are built into the RAM itself, and under software such as CPU-Z you can find out what settings your memory is capable of. It's a handy guide to understanding the best way to go about altering your timings in the BIOS since it will give you an idea of the range – lowest and highest – that the memory is capable of. Don't take it as fact, of course, since you can still tweak it to how you like, but it's good to check before any changes are made.

XMP settings – This is related to the SPD settings. As an alternative to JEDEC standard settings that are supplied with most memory, you can also get XMP settings. These are prescribed profiles for the RAM itself, which can be enabled in the BIOS to automatically overclock your memory for you. It's a safer option for those inexperienced or wary of overclocking memory since it will give the safe timings and frequency settings as designed by the manufacturer. Once you're more comfortable with overclocking, however, you might want to forgo this option in favour of your own tweaking to find the very best setting for your system. You can find these XMP settings in the SPD tab of CPU-Z.

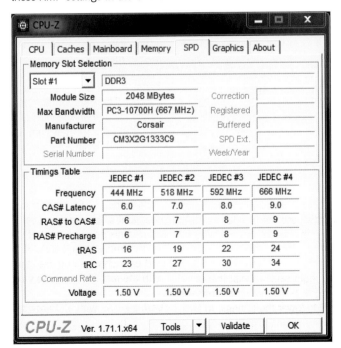

If you're not sure where to begin when it comes to RAM timing changes, you can check with the manufacturer's in-built SPD settings to see what kinds of ranges they suggest.

PART 6 Benchmarking and testing

It's important to remember that overclocking is a very gradual process, and even the most experienced overclockers must go through a regime of tweaking and testing to find the setting that they're most comfortable with. While overclocking can initially be quite a daunting task, providing you're vigilant about regular stress-tests and benchmarking then you'll deal easily with problems as they arise, and know exactly what previous state to revert to in order to make it work again. When overclocking your GPU, however, you've a number of benchmarking options available, and we wanted to devote some space to talking about the different software and why you might favour one over another. You should also remember that while an overclock might be 'benchmark stable', it might not be suitable when it comes to gaming. This is especially the case with GPUs, where the extra variable from your own input can put more strain on its calculations and processing. We've included some good suggestions for you to test your overclocked GPU, should you need it.

Benchmarking software

Futuremark 3DMark

3DMark is perhaps the most professional of the variants of benchmarking software, and as such it has made something of a name for itself as the go-to tool to test your system. 3DMark is designed specifically for 3D gaming, however, and will test everything from your GPU's ability to render models to how well it computes physics, lighting, particle effects and even other modern gaming techniques like volumetric fog. It's about as comprehensive as you can get, though lower-end cards will begin to struggle with frame rate towards the end. It'll even give you a calculated 3DMark 'score' upon completion, showing where your current system ranks in the grand scheme of things.

Unigine Heaven

The second most common benchmarking software is Unigine's Heaven, and it perhaps loses out to 3DMark due to the fact that its free, basic version isn't quite as feature-packed as 3DMark.

3DMark is the most popular benchmarking software, and rightly so. It stress-tests your GPU in every respect, from rendering to physics and lighting, as well as providing a 3DMark score for easy-to-understand ratings of where your GPU stands.

All the same, it's probably best to run each of these individually once you think you've settled on an overclock you're comfortable with just to ensure that you're getting results you can be pleased with. Both test the same elements, so it's really down to personal preference which you use when it comes to regular tests in-between overclocking changes.

FRAPS

There are two versions of FRAPS, free and paid-for. While the fairly cheap cost of the software brings with it some added benefits – especially if you hope to capture raw video footage – the free version is worth downloading for your own tests. It's

Unigine doesn't offer quite the same level of high-end testing as 3DMark does, but it's good to use in conjunction with other software to get a more complete benchmark test.

PlanetSide 2 is a very good looking game, but its huge open world engine means that it is also very demanding to run on Ultra settings; a good test for your machine.

worth noting that this isn't actually benchmarking software; instead it will display an up-to-date frame-rate counter over the games you play, making it imperative that you use this software while testing the capabilties of your GPU by playing the games themselves. Some players even get quite finicky about their frame rates and like to always keep it active while playing. It's a low demand on the system, so there's really no reason not to.

Games to test with

Crysis 3

Crytek has become something of a leader in pushing graphics cards to the limit, and while *Crysis 3* was fairly well optimised the game can be pushed to some serious lengths to create some scarily realistic vistas. Elements like tall swaying grass – which moves as you walk through it – and plenty of tricks of lighting make this a treat to witness in action. If you want to truly test your rig, this might be the way to go.

The Witcher 2: Enhanced Edition

As much as this game is a visual feast – what with all its colour and post-processing effects – the real benefit in using it to test your graphics card is its implementation of HDR (high-dynamic range) rendering. It isn't exclusively used in *The Witcher 2*, but it is the core reason that the game looks as bright and vibrant as it does. Plus, it's a pretty good RPG too.

PlanetSide 2

This is a huge, open-world massively multiplayer shooter, so adding that to some of the best graphics currently available on PC makes for a truly impressive piece of software. It's not

brilliantly optimised, either, which might sound like an issue but is actually a good way of testing what your PC can do. And best of all it's free to download and play, too, so won't cost you anything as a result.

Arma 3

Another large-scale, open-world FPS except this one is particularly interested in detail. That means a huge range of weapons, vehicles and character models and animations created with an uncanny level of detail. The game has a very heavy focus on simulation, too, so graphical elements such as volumetric clouds and realistic lighting all play a part in making the game feel as realistic as possible. Which, handily, makes it all the more demanding for testing your GPU.

Star Citizen

This is another game built on Crytek's Cryengine, and which as a result features a scary level of graphical detail and realism, even if it is set in space. It's not even a fully fledged game yet (even if you do need to pay to access it), but if you're something of a sci-fi nerd then you will definitely want to look at *Star Citizen* – exploring the hangar for your vessel is nothing less than spacecraft porn.

Hitman: Absolution

While this is certainly a very attractive game to look at, it's most impressive because of its use of crowds. Few games have matched this level of fidelity with such a large number of interactive non-player characters on screen either. In particular the Chinatown mission should be your target, which really pushes the numbers of on-screen graphical demands to the max.

Whether it's ogling your spacecraft in its hangar or taking it for a spin out in the vastness of space, *Star Citizen* always manages to look a real treat – making it a great test for your card.

7

PART **7**

Maintenance and settings

Even if you built your brand new gaming PC yourself, just like any piece of hardware it will fall victim to the tests of time. What this means is that your components will age and eventually – hopefully many years down the line – they will finally give up the ghost. Mercifully there are things you can do to help maintain your new PC, and it's highly recommended you do.

There are many ways you can keep your PC running as well as the day it was put together, whether it's clearing away the layers of dust from your PC's parts or making sure your hard drive is free of clutter and unwanted files. There are things you can alter in the settings of your games, too, that will allow you to make the most of your hardware, even when it is beginning to age beyond advancements in computing technology. There's an art to maintaining a PC and it does require a bit of willpower; none of this will be fun to do, but if you set aside just an hour or so a month to keep on top of potential problems then you'll be able to keep your PC fit and healthy for much longer. And, of course, eventually a time will come when you'll need to look for upgrades to your machine to help keep your gaming as high fidelity as possible. Luckily this section will help you through all that.

PART

Maintaining your hardware

When it comes to maintenance of your PC hardware there are, thankfully, only a couple of things you need to do. Frankly, providing everything's installed properly, there are no reasons why your hardware should have shifted at all. If you move your PC regularly the wires might need poking back into out of the way places, but besides that the hardware you install doesn't need much special treatment.

With that said, however, there is one major threat: dust. It's an unavoidable problem, sadly, and one that requires a great deal of effort in ensuring the build up isn't ever too much. Dust will increase the temperature that your parts run at, with your cooling fans struggling to move cool air around as effectively and hardware such as your graphics card insulating itself – thus running hotter the longer it is under load. You can use the following steps as often as you think necessary, but we'd recommend a poke around your machine perhaps once a month to keep an eye on any dust build up, but leave it no more than six months. Any longer than that and the dust will become harder and harder to clean off.

Then there is the thermal paste on your CPU, a process that can be quite intimidating for first-timers. If you find your CPU is becoming incredibly hot and perhaps even dramatically affecting the stability of your PC then it might be time to clean up the thermal paste between your air cooler and the CPU chip. Some recommend replacing the thermal paste about once a year – and there are benefits to that – but providing you're not overclocking your machine you should be okay to leave the stock paste on there for a couple of years at least.

Necessary equipment

Compressed air
A can of compressed air is easily bought from any hardware store and is the safest most efficient way of cleaning dust off computer parts. Only use short bursts when using compressed air, since longer blasts could result in condensation. Alternatively you can use a powered air blower, which functions in the same way.

Static-free cloth
These special cloths are safe to use on computer parts since they won't fry your hardware with any accidental static electricity. You won't want to use this to clean every part of your machine but it

You can buy cans of compressed air for next to nothing at practically any hardware store. It's great for cleaning in-between keyboard keys too.

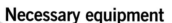

can give you a more effective means of removal on flat surfaces – such as the casing on graphics cards – that can become more heavily caked in dust. Absolutely do not attempt to clean any part of your PC with a cloth if it isn't static-free.

Vacuum

You won't want to use a full-powered vacuum on the inside of your PC – the static and power involved would be incredibly damaging for your PC. However using the nozzle will be important for cleaning up all that dust later on, and if you can get a weaker hand-vacuum you'll find it's great for gathering that pesky dust.

Cleaning away dust

Start by unplugging all the cables from your PC, and place it on a flat surface – standing is fine in this case, since dust will simply fall back onto the motherboard if it is lying flat. Remove any side panels you have, both if your case has two. At this point take note of any cables. Though they should already be tidied away, it's good to check and make sure they won't cause any accidents with your hardware. If they aren't already, use cable ties to tidy away any loose cables.

Using a can of compressed air, blow on each of the parts to dislodge any dust. Do this at an angle but fairly close so as to ensure the dust flies out away from the case. Pay particular attention to each of your PC's fans, the power supply unit (this is imperative) and any extra cards installed into the PCI slots – such as your graphics card.

If you haven't much space in your case you can consider removing the power supply unit and its connected cables. This will free up a large chunk of space to get a better angle, and will make it easier to clear away any dust from parts blocked by the cables themselves. Remember to wipe the cables clean too using the static-free cloth.

The motherboard itself should be relatively free of dust – providing it is positioned upright, as is the situation for most cases. All the same, give it a spray across the whole motherboard from about three or four inches away to knock off any dust.

If you have a smaller nozzle to attach, do so and use that to blow away any dust in between the small crevices – such as between the memory bays or around the CPU area. Make sure you're thorough with this nozzle, since it will focus the air a lot more intensely.

Finally use your static-free cloth for very gentle strokes across flat surfaces and hard edges, such as the top of your graphics card, storage drives or the edges of your RAM and fans. The base of the case, now, will likely need dusting too, and if you removed the PSU it'll be easier to clean. Be gentle here, only use a small portion of the cloth at a time and don't use this to clean the motherboard or chips on parts like the graphics card; the cloth could easily get snagged on something and cause damage.

Replacing thermal paste

■ If you find your CPU becoming unreasonably hot during use, it might be time to consider replacing the thermal paste between your CPU chip and the motherboard. Some recommend replacing this paste once every twelve months, but if you're inexperienced it's better to leave well alone until you find problems with your CPU unexpectedly affecting performance.

■ You'll need to remove any fans installed onto the CPU, whether that is the stock fan that comes with the chip or any aftermarket installation you've opted for. Leave the CPU installed, but first you'll want to clean the heatsink on the fan.

■ Clean away the existing thermal paste on the heatsink. Use a flat edge, such as an old credit card or a business card, to wipe the majority of the paste away and then use isopropyl alcohol and a cloth to wipe away the remaining paste. Make sure all of the paste has been removed.

■ Now repeat the process for the CPU, again making sure you keep it installed in the motherboard. Use isopropyl alcohol to ensure the CPU is completely free of old thermal paste.

■ Now apply new thermal paste, which can be bought in most hardware stores or online very easily. Squeeze roughly a pea-sized amount of thermal paste onto the centre of the CPU and then place and reattach the heatsink squarely on top to spread the paste evenly across the back of the chip. Don't try to spread it yourself, since it needs to remain even.

■ Some thermal pastes require specific methods of application, so simply refer to the instructions with your product to ensure you apply it correctly.

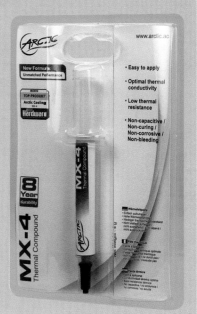

Thermal paste comes in all shapes and sizes, but it's not too complicated. The Arctic range is generally the most popular.

PART

Maintaining the software

It's somewhat ironic that physically cleaning your PC is much less tiresome than doing so digitally. Through natural use of your computer it will, inevitably, become a little untidy. Whether you use it primarily for gaming or not, your PC's software will become filled with redundant programs, duplicate files and folders and even leftover temporary installation files. It's an inevitability, really, and all this excess can slow your PC down, not dramatically at first but if you don't keep the spring cleaning up you'll find it will eventually have a noticeable effect on your PC's performance.

What you need to do, then, is make a point of cleaning up your software whenever you can. It doesn't have to be a strict, regular thing but you may find it becomes something of a habit to follow these few steps once a month or so, and in doing so you'll make sure your PC never becomes bogged down with data. It could be worth taking this time to also backup any important data or files you

If you're never going to play a game again, you may as well uninstall it – even if the space it takes up is inconsequential.

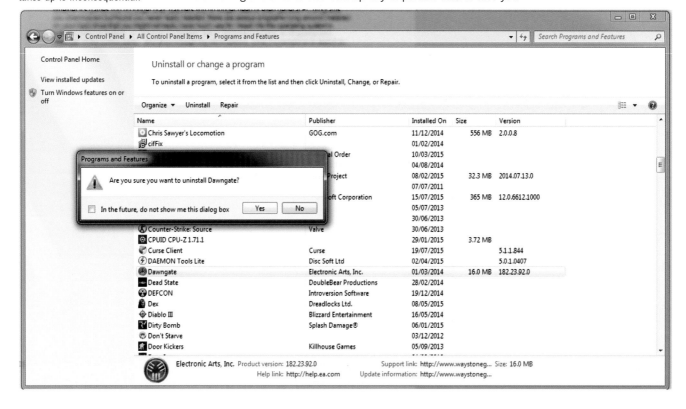

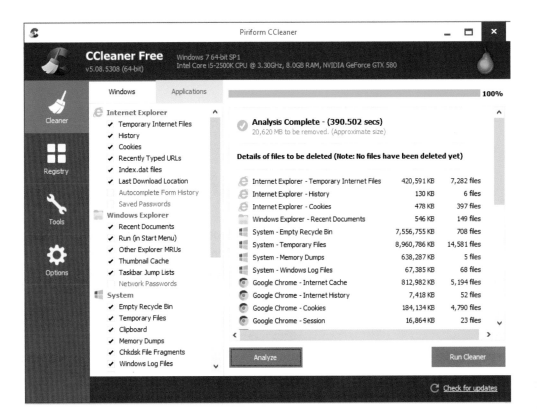

might have installed on your hard drive; as sad as it is to say, hard drive failures can happen to even the most organised of PC users. Follow these few tips every so often, however, and your PC will remain as streamlined as the day you made it.

Uninstall unwanted software

Whether it's games you no longer play, patchers you no longer need or even general PC programs you downloaded but found you never really needed, there are always programs lying around installed on your hard drive that you might not really have much use for. Head into the operating system's software removal feature – in Windows it is termed 'Add or Remove programs' or 'Programs and Features' in the control panel – and scroll through the list of options. While it is beneficial to search by size, if you're doing a spot of cleaning it might be better to search alphabetically, where you can take a better look at the programs themselves. Any you don't use – or use very rarely – can be uninstalled, freeing up space and removing any would-be memory usage. Remember you can always locate the folder where the program's files are installed and look for an executable that will remove the files for you.

Use CCleaner

It might seem somewhat counterproductive to download software to clean up your software, but there are some – such as the very popular CCleaner – that help greatly in the battle against messy machines. You can use CCleaner for a wide number of your software maintenance needs, but its real benefit is its 'Cleaner' option where you can easily – in one menu – remove any unwanted, temporary or duplicate files. It's great for ease of use, and can even let you check the files you want cleaned away and the files you don't. There are many other programs out there that claim to offer the same benefits of CCleaner, some even claiming

CCleaner is your all-in-one software cleanup tool, and can help with every aspect of hard drive spring cleaning.

to 'enhance the performance of your PC', but in truth there are many that are little more than glorified software removal programs or perhaps even malware. Stick with CCleaner; it's the most popular for a reason and will do everything you need very well.

Clear caches, download folder and desktop

While CCleaner can help with many of these functions, it's worth drawing attention to the importance of it. Temporary files and cached data is the biggest threat to PC performance because it is information that is quite regularly referenced and re-referenced by software that you use often – in particular your internet browser – even if that data is old and no longer needed. Clearing out your history, cached files and temporary files will improve performance since there won't be quite as much information that your CPU and memory needs to take note of. Again, CCleaner is great for helping with this. Outside of that it's worth checking any folders that might naturally accrue files that eventually become old and irrelevant, such as your Downloads, Documents and Pictures folders. Find these folders and go through the files inside to delete those you don't need. Repeat the process for your desktop, which can – for many – become something of a dumping ground for shortcuts and downloaded files. And don't forget to clear your recycling bin out once you've done all this.

Go through defragmentation

Hard drives – by their very nature – can become a little confused. With so much data writing and rewriting going on in even a single session on your PC, months of use can cause your files to become fragmented, slowing your PC down as it has to search for information in a wider number of places. It's a healthy process to go through defragmentation to analyse your hard drives and recalibrate the data so it can be more easily found. There are a number of software options out there that help with defragmentation, but if you're running Windows you'll likely find that the basic tool pre-installed onto your system will be more than enough to proceed with this step. Either way it's good to defragment your hard drive perhaps three or four times a year.

Cancel launch start-up programs

Having numerous programs that boot up at the same time as your operating system can slow down your PC; you've likely used an old PC before that needs a few minutes to 'settle' before it can be properly used – that's the resultant effect of the menace of start-up software. Some you will want booting up alongside your PC – such as antivirus software – but in truth there are many times where it can be better to cancel many of the programs that do start-up on launch. Again, CCleaner can help with this (we did say it was useful!) but if you don't fancy using that you can do it yourself with Windows. In the start menu search for 'msconfig', open the program and then select 'Startup'. Here you'll see all the programs that are attempting to boot up alongside Windows, simply uncheck the ones you don't need (or don't want to start up until you need them) and then click 'Apply'. Job done.

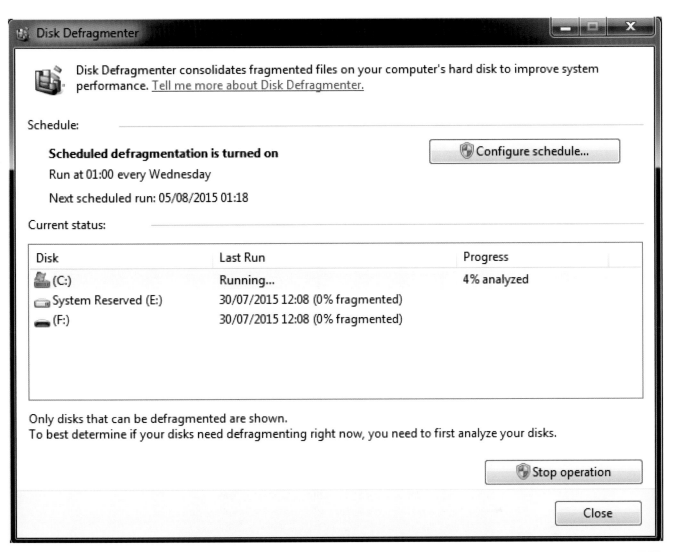

It's good to go through defragmentation every so often, if only so it keeps your hard drive running as smoothly as possible.

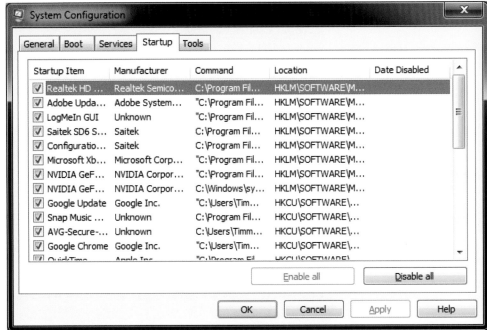

After a year or two, you may be surprised to find so many programs starting up alongside Windows. You won't need all of them.

PART  Upgrading existing parts

There's no avoiding the onset of age, and technology is no different. When it comes to your PC, the amount of time it can survive before it becomes obsolete is entirely dependant on the initial build. If you've spent over £1,000 to make sure your PC is a top-of-the-line piece of kit then you can be sure that – barring any unexpected faults with any given part – it'll last you a good few years running games at their very best. Eventually it will come to a point when enough is enough, however, and you may not want to simply start all over again. That would be costly, more than anything else.

At this point you'll need to figure out what hardware it is you need to replace – and in all likelihood it'll be the graphics card first – and then you'll need to figure out what it is you can upgrade it with. This follows the same sorts of stipulations that you would've had when originally buying the hardware, which is to say ensuring they match certain criteria with the motherboard, case and other compatible parts. Providing you fulfil these criteria you'll be okay to upgrade whichever part you want, following the same procedures listed in the 'Build a gaming PC' section. We don't need to cover that again since the process is the same (except you're removing the existing part first), so instead we'll explain how to know which part to upgrade, and what to upgrade it with.

Your system memory is the quickest, easiest and cheapest upgrade you can go for – but make sure you only buy RAM with the same channel setup as your motherboard.

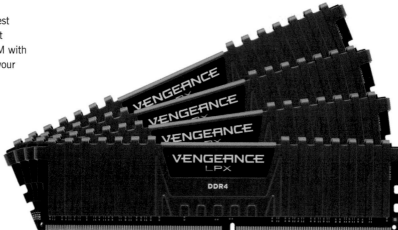

Because of the standardised nature of PC hardware these days it's often very simple upgrading different parts, even the likes of GPUs. Make sure the upgrades are compatible, however.

When to upgrade your graphics card

For PC gamers the most integral part of their gaming experience is the graphics card. This is the piece of hardware that creates the visuals for your games, and if that is not able to perform as well as it used to it will leave your games stuttering under the weight of their graphical prowess. At what point you deem it important to upgrade your GPU comes down to entirely what standard you want to play your games at. You can gradually lower the settings in-game, for example, to extend the life of the GPU by playing games with inferior graphical options activated. It means you won't be able to enjoy games at their absolute best, but you'll get a good few months out of the card itself. Once it becomes a struggle to find a balance between a visual fidelity you're happy with and a consistent, stable frame rate then you know it's time to upgrade. Frame rate is the most important aspect, since making sure that is steady allows for a more enjoyable experience. With regards to what you should upgrade with, well that comes largely down to what is considered to be the 'best' at the time. Thankfully GPUs tend to follow a fairly familiar pattern, so if you spent £300 on a card initially then look to spend the same the second time around – you'll roughly get something in the same ballpark, in terms of comparative power – that you had previously.

When to upgrade your memory

RAM is often the easiest upgrade to go for. If you find your machine is taking a while to load or struggling when multitasking programs – such as switching between a fullscreen game and the Steam program – then it's often easier to upgrade your RAM rather than anything else. It's only a temporary fix since there are far more important parts – at least when it comes to the speed of your computer – than the memory, but it's also a fairly low-cost upgrade too. You'll likely be looking at a cost of around £100 to upgrade your memory rather than the £300–400 for any other

more significant piece of hardware, so it's an easy switch. Just make sure that if you do upgrade your RAM, do so with the exact same memory as before (if you're adding to it) or, preferably, a completely new set. Be sure to follow our tips on buying memory at the front of the book to know how best to proceed when buying RAM.

When to upgrade your CPU

It's tougher to detect when a CPU is holding back your gaming performance, especially since modern games often rely more heavily on your graphics card's capabilities. Finding out which part is causing the bottleneck is difficult, but since the CPU handles logical computation then testing it out with the latest strategy game (or anything with a lot of complex AI, really) will help; if it takes much longer than it should then, chances are, it's your CPU. However, you don't want to shell out another £300 for a 'chance' that your CPU is the problem; in this case download and install HWMonitor, a piece of software that will calculate a percentage of your hardware's capacities and how close it is to its maximum. When upgrading, however, you need to be very certain that the CPU you're buying has the same socket as your motherboard, and in all likelihood you'll need to buy a new motherboard too. If your PC is older than two years, then you'll probably need to upgrade the motherboard, so be sure to check out the compatibility.

When to upgrade your storage

This is probably the only upgrade situation that is guided more by your own personal preference than technical limits. If you find your hard drive is getting full and you're having to regularly juggle installed games, then it might be time to upgrade your storage. The beauty of upgrading your hard drive, however, is the fact that you have numerous options. You can combine a second hard drive alongside your older one to run two storages drives, with one acting as a sort of dumping ground. Alternatively you could swap it out entirely for a much larger equivalent, and use the older hard drive as a backup storage drive (you can actually buy cases to turn an existing drive into a portable storage drive). Or you might decide to splash out for a quicker, more efficient solid state drive (SSD), which by the time you need to upgrade will have reduced even

Cooling options are important for the longevity of your PC, but if you're considering overclocking you should also make sure your PC's temperature will stay down.

more in price with much larger capacities available. Remember, however, that though your hard drive might seem sufficient for now, the older a HDD gets the more likely it is to fail – for the safety of all your stored data it can often be better to pre-empt any failure if your drive is three or four years old.

When to upgrade your cooling

Providing you've not had any temperature problems with your system since its installation – and truth be told, there's no reason why you ought to – then the only reason you might need to upgrade your current cooling system is when you make a change to the hardware in your PC. This could be swapping a GPU out for a much more powerful and power-hungry equivalent, for example, or maybe you've been tempted by our guide on overclocking. In either case, if you're increasing the overall power consumption of your machine then you may also be increasing the running temperature, and at this point the cooling system you have might not be adequate. Use software to check the running temperature of your various parts when under strain to check this is the case, though – if something is getting too hot – it will likely be noticeable in performance drops anyway. When upgrading you'll need to think about what options are open to you. Once upon a time people would cut holes into side panels and install secondary or tertiary fans, but these days a single upgrade to the existing fan should be enough. If not, then consider water cooling as your last option before ultimately resorting to underclocking (or resetting) the running capabilities of your CPU, GPU or memory.

PART 7

In-game settings explained

PC gaming is replete with often hundreds of little settings and tweaks that can be made to a game to make it run optimally on your machine. Since every PC is different – from the hardware installed to the active, running software – it's impossible for developers to create games that can run exactly the same across all forms of PC hardware. It works on consoles because the hardware is always the same, it's predictable; on PCs more work needs to be done to enable as wide a range of users as possible. That's where the visual settings come in, letting you tweak a game's options to make it run as smoothly as possible with as high a fidelity as possible on whatever tier of build your PC is.

Now if you'd rather not get into the nitty gritty of tailoring settings for your needs then more often than not there is a set of options to pick from, usually with 'Ultra' at the top-end and 'Low' at the bottom. These are sets of generic changes to the settings, and will suffice for those who can't be bothered tinkering with the settings. However, there's also a wide range of options and though the ones that are available differ from game to game, their meanings never change. There is a lot of jargon involved here, so we're going to bust that all wide open and explain a little bit about what it is these different settings change and why they are important. Remember: not all of these will be in every game, and there may well be some game-specific options too – such as character model quality. Use your own judgment in this regard, but note that post-processing effects often have a greater impact on your processing than high polygon counts.

Here's an example of screen tearing, an often unavoidable problem that can be resolved by enabling VSync.

Type of setting	What it affects	Details
Resolution	The number of pixels – and therefore clarity of the image – that is rendered onto your monitor.	Resolution is important for the visual fidelity, and ideally you'll render a game to match that of your monitor's resolution (probably 1080p or 1440p). However it is also possible to render higher than your monitor's resolution, which will be downscaled to fit the screen and provide even greater detail.
VSync	Locks the frame rate to either 30 or 60 frames per second.	Some games struggle rendering fast moving actions – such as camera control – and this can result in screen-tearing. Enabling Vertical Synchronisation prevents any erratic frame-rate fluctuations to eliminate this.
Adaptive VSync	The same as VSync, but disables itself when dropping below 60 frames per second.	With VSync, if a frame rate drops below 60FPS it will then switch to 30FPS – but if this happens often it can cause stuttering. NVIDIA's Adaptive VSync stops this by switching VSync off if the frame rate drops below 60FPS.
View distance	Controls the distance that is rendered.	This might be obvious, but by controlling the distance at which the game world is rendered you can better control your PC's performance. The game world is not completely rendered, and is instead only rendered when it comes into view – this option controls the distance that occurs at.
Field of view	Controls the 'wideness' of your character's view.	Popular in first-person games, field of view lets you alter the angle at which the camera – or your character – is able to see. On wider monitors this can create a much more realistic viewpoint, and give you a greater vision while playing. Useful for multiplayer games.
GSync/Freesync	With a compatible monitor this can alter the screen's refresh rate to match the frame rate.	As relatively new technology (NVIDIA has GSync, AMD has Freesync) there aren't all that many cases where this is possible, but if you have a compatible GPU and monitor, it will remove any screen tearing and input lag issues with VSync.
Texture quality	Controls the resolution of in-game textures.	Though not always, you can sometimes control the quality of textures – naturally improving performance if opting for lower-quality textures.
Bilinear/Trilinear Filtering	Affects the way 2D images – or textures – are displayed on a 3D model from different angles.	Filtering helps keep control of the way textures work on 3D models, and bilinear is the most basic method of this. Trilinear is better, but only in that it takes samples from nearby textures too.
Anisotropic Filtering	Affects the way 2D images – or textures – are displayed on a 3D model from different angles.	This is a stronger form of filtering that takes into account many more factors. It requires more processing power, of course, but enables greater clarity at further ranges. Better for avoiding blurriness of textures at longer distances.
Anti-aliasing (MSAA – Multisampling)	Smooths hard edges of pixels for a more natural appearance.	MSAA – or multisampling anti-aliasing – is the basic form of AA for videogames, offers decent results with good efficiency. A higher the number before this means more accuracy at a higher cost on your CPU and GPU.
Anti-aliasing (CSAA – Coverage sampling)	Smooths hard edges of pixels for a more natural appearance.	This is NVIDIA's version of MSAA, and provides the same results with greater efficiency. A higher the number before this means more accuracy at a higher cost on your CPU and GPU.
Anti-aliasing (CFAA – Custom filter)	Smooths hard edges of pixels for a more natural appearance.	This is AMD's version of MSAA, a more efficient version of the aliasing with similar results. A higher the number before this means more accuracy at a higher cost on your CPU and GPU.
Anti-aliasing (FXAA – Fast approximate)	Smooths hard edges of pixels for a more natural appearance.	As the name suggests, this anti-aliasing is a quick-action version. Rather than analyse different models, FXAA instead applies a post-processing filter to smooth the entire scene. A higher the number before this means more accuracy at a higher cost on your CPU and GPU.

Type of setting	What it affects	Details
Anti-aliasing (MLAA – Morphological)	Smooths hard edges of pixels for a more natural appearance.	A form of AA unique to AMD cards. This uses a unique algorithm to detect jagged edges in an entire frame/scene, and smooths it out. A higher the number before this means more accuracy at a higher cost on your CPU and GPU.
Anti-aliasing (SMAA – Enhanced Subpixel Morphological)	Smooths hard edges of pixels for a more natural appearance.	An enhanced version of MLAA that also utilises methods of MSAA. A higher the number before this means more accuracy at a higher cost on your CPU and GPU.
Anti-aliasing (TXAA – Temporal)	Smooths hard edges of pixels for a more natural appearance.	Utilises MSAA techniques with other filters, while using existing frame AA data to compute the next frame. A higher the number before this means more accuracy at a higher cost on your CPU and GPU.
Anti-aliasing (MFAA – Multi-frame)	Smooths hard edges of pixels for a more natural appearance.	Exclusively to NVIDIA's new Maxwell range, MFAA allows more customisable patterns of anti-aliasing. A higher the number before this means more accuracy at a higher cost on your CPU and GPU.
Ambient occlusion (SSAO)	Attempts to display lighting in a more realistic fashion.	As a process-heavy option, SSAO can be one of the first you can disable. It can help to make lighting look more realistic since it attempts to calculate which parts of a scene should have less light than another.
Bloom	Exaggerates lighting for a stronger visual appearance.	Bloom is more of an artistic element, and is most notable for having the light render more intensely, appearing to spill out over the edges of windows and the like. Sometimes it helps create a unique visual cue, but can often be disabled.
Depth of field	Visual effect to make distant or peripheral vision blurred.	Depth of field is a post-processing effect that draws attention to centralised objects while additional details appear blurred. As a post-processing effect, this is often superfluous and can be disabled.
Detail quality	Controls the quality of particular details.	This can often take any form, sometimes simply called 'Detail' other times with greater specificity, such as 'Grass/Foliage detail'. This is often referring to more minute elements of a game, however, and can be one of the first adjustments you need to make.
HDR (High dymanic range) lighting	Improves the range of detail from light areas to darkened areas.	HDR is a very process-heavy feature that can be disabled first if your PC is beginning to age. A higher range allows for better detail in the darkest and lightest parts of a scene.
Shadow quality	Controls the overall quality of shadows.	As a superfluous graphical option, shadows can often be controlled – as with textures – to better match your hardware. Lower quality provides better performance.
Motion blur	Adds blurring to camera movements.	For a more cinematic feel, this post-processing effect replicates the way a camera processes movement – namely blurring pixels to give the impression of speed or movement.
Particle effects	Controls the strength, quality or regularity of particle effects.	Particle effects are often superfluous extras that help make a scene feel more realistic, such as dust mites floating in a beam of light or dirt being kicked up off the ground during a fight. Some games give you the option to customise these elements in a number of ways.
PhysX	Adds more realistic physics-based actions.	PhysX controls a game's ability to render realistic physics-based reactions – such as debris flying away after a devastating blow. It is often a toggleable option.

PART  Testing and fault-finding

So your new PC is dead. You've finished the build, closed the case, patted yourself on the back, turned on the power and … nothing. Not a peep.

This is a terrible moment in anyone's life and it is entirely natural to feel that heart-wrenching sinking feeling. We're here to help you solve your problems, but first let's lay down a couple of pointers. These aren't exactly rules or directions, but do please think of them as well-intentioned advice.

The first point is not to panic. Second, if in doubt wait it out. If you're British, stop and make a cup of tea. You may well have a problem or even a number of problems, but you don't want to make things worse, so take a step back and have a nice cup of tea (other beverages are available). Third, take nothing for granted. Make no assumptions. Always return to first principles. That sounds like three points, but it is actually the same thing said three ways. One of the fatal mistakes when you are fault-finding is to say: 'I have confirmed that part A works and that part B works so it follows that part C is faulty.' You need to be scientific. The truly cautious person will say: 'I think I have confirmed that part A works and it appears that part B works so it follows that part C is possibly faulty.' Fourth, avoid tunnel vision and keep your eyes wide open. The following tale may be just that, but it happens. Many years ago, back when we had telephones with a dial in the middle, an office worker phoned an IT support line: 'Hello, my computer is dead.'

The support guy walked through their script and asked the office person to check a few things. 'Can you look round the back of the computer and check the VGA cable is secure at both the PC and the monitor.'

'No I cannot do that,' came the reply, 'I can't see anything as the power cut has taken out the lights.'

PART

Troubleshooting

Let's assume you've built your PC, turned it on for the first time ... and nothing happens. You can't get into BIOS, let alone install Windows. How and where do you begin to troubleshoot?

In fact, identifying a problem at this stage is very much easier than down the road when you've got a printer, scanner, webcam and goodness knows what other hardware attached; not to mention 57 software programs doing their utmost to interfere with one another, a real risk of viruses and perhaps a utility suite that does more harm than good. Your computer will never be so easy to diagnose and cure as it is right now.

Check the cables

The very first step is all too obvious but all too often overlooked: check that all external cables are securely connected in the correct places:

☐ The computer's PSU should be plugged into a mains wall socket (or power gangplank).

☐ So should the monitor.

☐ The mains electricity supply should be turned on at the wall.

☐ The monitor should be connected to the video card's VGA, DVI or HDMI output.

☐ The keyboard should be connected to the computer's PS/2-style keyboard port (not to a USB port, unless USB support has already been enabled in BIOS, and not to the mouse port).

☐ The PSU should be set to the correct voltage and turned on.

Now turn on the monitor. A power indication LED on the monitor housing should illuminate and, hopefully, you'll see something on the screen. If not, re-read the monitor manual and double-check that you've correctly identified the on/off switch and are not busy fiddling with the brightness or contrast controls. It's not always obvious which switch is which. If the power light still does not come on, it sounds like the monitor itself may be at fault. Try changing the fuse in the cable. Ideally, test the monitor with another PC.

Internal inspection

Now turn on the PC itself. Press the large on/off switch on the front of the case, not the smaller reset switch. You should hear the whirring of internal fans and either a single beep or a sequence of beeps. But let's assume that all seems lifeless. Again, check/change the fuse in the PSU power cable. If this doesn't help, unplug all cables, including the monitor, take off the case covers

The modular design of modern PSUs is superb but adds a load of extra connections that can cause problems.

and lay the computer on its side. Now systematically check every internal connection. Again, here's a quick checklist to tick off:

- ☐ The PSU should be connected to the motherboard with a large 24-pin plug and also, if appropriate, with ATX 12V and ATX Auxiliary cables.
- ☐ The heatsink fan should be plugged into a power socket on the motherboard.
- ☐ The case fans should be likewise connected.
- ☐ All drives should be connected to the appropriate sockets on the motherboard with ribbon cables.
- ☐ All drives should be connected to the PSU with power cables.
- ☐ The graphics card should be securely sited in its AGP or PCI Express slot.
- ☐ All other expansion cards should be likewise in place.
- ☐ Look for loose screws inside the case, lest one should be causing a short circuit.
- ☐ Check the front panel connections. If the case's on/off switch is disconnected from the motherboard, you won't be able to start the system.
- ☐ Are any cables snagging on fans?
- ☐ Are the retention clips on the memory DIMMs fully closed?
- ☐ Does anything on the motherboard look obviously broken or damaged?

Disconnect each cable in turn and look for bent pins on the plugs and sockets. These can usually be straightened with small, pointy pliers and a steady hand. Reconnect everything, including the monitor and power cable, and turn the computer on once more. Leave the covers off to aid observation. Does it now burst into life as if by magic? Rather gallingly, unplugging and replacing a cable is sometimes all it takes to fix an elusive but strictly temporary glitch.

PSU problems

Look for an LED on the motherboard (check the manual for its location). This should illuminate whenever the PSU is connected to the mains power and turned on, even when the computer itself is off. The LED confirms that the motherboard is receiving power; if it stays dark, the PSU itself may be at fault.

When you turn on the computer, do the fans remain static? Does the CD drive disc tray refuse to open? Is all depressingly dead? This would confirm the PSU as the problem. Use an alternative power cable, perhaps borrowed from the monitor, just to be sure. If still nothing happens, remove and replace the PSU.

NEVER TRY TO OPEN OR REPAIR A PSU. Nor should you try running it while it's disconnected from the motherboard, as a PSU can only operate with a load.

Finding a connection fault

By now your should be reasonably confident that you have mains power arriving at the input of your PSU. Until a few years ago, the fact that mains power arrived at the PSU pretty much guaranteed that 12V, 5V and 3.3V would flow to the motherboard, graphics card and SSD, and if it didn't then you could be confident the PSU was faulty.

The rise of the modular PSU changed all that. While the modular PSU with its detachable cables looks much neater than the messy old PSUs from the past, this change introduces a load of new connection points.

The simple rule of thumb is that if a plug fits in a socket you are safe to use it, but it makes sense to read the legends printed on the cables and PSU just to make sure you have the right thing in the right place. There is a good chance that the cables will all appear to be properly connected, but you need to be sure you hear that satisfying click as you push them into place. If you have any doubts, give each cable a gentle tug to ensure it is secure.

No doubt you have carefully routed the PSU cables inside your PC so that they feed around the back of the motherboard tray and, inevitably, make some twists and turns en route to

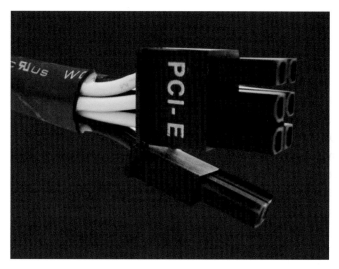

If you haven't got enough power heading to your graphics card(s), you can expect to hit problems.

This EVGA Z87 Stinger is a prime example of a motherboard that sports a number of premium features such as micro buttons and a debug display.

their destination. If you have any doubt in your mind, it is best to make direct connections and simply feed the cables across the motherboard. You can always tidy it up once you have fixed your problems, but for the moment you simply need power and, of course, to ensure the cables are clear of any fans.

Power supply to your graphics card is a slightly vexing issue. You don't need much power to start Windows running and get the desktop displayed on your monitor, but every graphics card on the market insists that you connect those dratted 6-pin and 8-pin connectors before the system will even think of starting. Ideally, if you are using a CPU or APU that contains a graphics core, you would temporarily remove your graphics card(s) to take them out of the equation.

Power On Self Test (POST)

The photo of this EVGA Z87 Stinger Mini-ITX motherboard (opposite) shows three things of interest. At the bottom right we have the front panel header connections, at the top right there is the POST debug display and at the top there are Power and Reset buttons. These are premium features that you won't find on mainstream and budget motherboards, but hopefully you have aimed high with your gaming PC build. The colour-coded front panel headers make life much easier when you connect the Power and Reset buttons along with the Power and Activity LEDs. These connections are all interchangeable and it is alarmingly easy to plug things together incorrectly or even to miss the header and only engage with one pin rather than two. If you make that mistake, you can press the Power button all you like and your perfectly functioning PC will refuse to respond. The same thing applies if the wiring to the front of the case is damaged or the button is faulty.

Using the Power micro buttons bypasses this problem entirely. If you don't have micro buttons on your motherboard, the time-honoured alternative is to use a plain screwdriver to short the two header pins. Under no circumstances short the pins with a jumper to make a permanent connection – this is a momentary connection that sends a signal to the PSU to get things started. As you probably know, if you press and hold the Power button for ten seconds when your PC is running you will actually force it to shut down.

The other advantage of a premium motherboard is the POST code debug display. During POST (Power On Self Test) the display shows a series of two character codes that you can interpret to see the progress of your system start-up. and we've posted the most popular codes later in this section.

With a premium motherboard you can tell in moments whether or not you have power and whether the power button is attempting to boot your new PC into life. With a lesser motherboard you are pretty much in the dark between the time the fans start turning and when the reassuring Windows logo appears on your screen.

PART 8 Finding faulty hardware

If you still have a dead PC then the time has come to search for faulty hardware. Sadly if you've made sure every piece of hardware is properly installed, there are no faults with your power supply and that the PSU is correctly connected to every necessary part, well ... that means you've got a faulty piece of hardware somewhere. It could be as simple as a mistake in the installation, though, so don't despair too much.

If you have previously run the hardware you will have hopefully tracked down the installation problem by the simple procedure of retracing your steps. If you haven't and you are utterly stumped then pull the motherboard assembly from the case and give it a try. It is so much quicker and easier to check components when you have good access and a PC case can be a tough working environment. Check each of the following processes one by one to try and locate your issue.

Installing your new hardware in a case can introduce all sorts of unexpected problems, even if you use high-end hardware such as this Phanteks Enthoo Pro.

■ The most obvious candidate is the CPU socket on your Intel motherboard as the CPU is effectively flat and sits on a series of 1,150 tiny springs that make contact. The CPU package has a couple of notches that engage with the socket on the motherboard and provided you carefully rest it in place then all is well. It only takes a tiny slip and you can drop the CPU on to the motherboard, which can end up causing all sorts of damage. You then have to make a decision about returning the motherboard, attempting to fix the damage or buying a replacement.

■ AMD customers are in a slightly different position as AMD uses the traditional approach where the CPU carries the pins while the socket is on the motherboard. You are most unlikely to damage the motherboard when you insert the CPU, but it is quite easy to bend a number of pins unless you line up the CPU quite precisely.

■ If you have done something utterly silly such as installing your DDR3 memory the wrong way round then you won't have been able to secure the latches. If you tried something a bit more subtle such as installing DDR2 memory in a DDR3 motherboard (or vice versa) then it either won't fit or the latches won't secure. This hardware has been designed to avoid precisely this problem so if the thing won't go in the slot there is a good reason.

■ It is perfectly possible that you have failed to correctly insert a graphics card in its PCI Express slot. You'll feel like an idiot, but we have all done it and the galling thing is that a graphics card can appear to be inserted correctly when it actually requires another push to seat it correctly. Most motherboards have a latch or some sort of locking mechanism to secure the end of the card that sits in the middle of the PC.

■ The two snags you need to watch for are the motherboard mounts and the expansion slots in the case. You need to be sure that the motherboard sits flat on its mounts, which are usually a set of metal posts that screw into holes in the side of the case. There is scope in a budget case for these holes to be out of line or for the mounting posts to have some variation, which throws out the alignment of the graphics card.

Searching for incompatibility

Having tackled the problems of broken components, loose connections and a lack of power, we move on to the tricky stuff.

Incompatible components can stop you in your tracks or, if you are particularly unfortunate, they can cause problems every once in a while at seemingly random moments. One giveaway is when you press the Power button and the fans rotate slightly in a sort of lurch and then immediately stop. It is obvious the PC is showing signs of life yet clearly it isn't going to burst into action.

PC technology runs on industry standards, which is why you can buy your case, PSU, motherboard, graphics card and cooling system from an array of vendors and have every confidence they will work together. Despite a colossal amount of hard work by the industry, you can run into problems, in particular with

your CPU and memory. Your motherboard supports a particular type of processor, but it may well not support every CPU that will fit in the socket. As mentioned in the Anatomy chapter, some AMD AM3+ CPUs require more power than you get from the earlier AM3 socket so if you put the later CPU in an earlier motherboard, it simply won't work.

A more common problem is to find that a motherboard built in, say, September 2014 supports CPUs made up to that point but requires a BIOS update for a CPU that was released in December 2014. You buy motherboard and CPU in January 2015 and find the hardware is incompatible and, humorously, you cannot start the system to update the BIOS. Certain motherboards get round this problem in ingenious ways. Intel offered a number of different methods to update the BIOS on its Intel-branded motherboards including from CD and would allow you to boot into the BIOS to perform the necessary update. Asus has gone a step further with its Republic of Gamers models that support USB BIOS flashback where you can update the BIOS from a flash drive on a bare motherboard that doesn't even have a CPU installed. Let's hope this concept spreads to all manufacturers.

Damaged components are a nightmare. The question is did you break it or can you claim on the warranty?

Incompatible memory is the stuff of nightmares and can cause endless problems, including an apparently dead PC.

Sometimes it can be tricky making the correct connection to your graphics card.

Memory support should be as easy as easy can be. Your motherboard supports DDR3, the CPU memory controller supports DDR3-2,133MHz and you buy some DDR3-1,600MHz. It is natural to expect the memory would fit and work and while it will only run at 1,600MHz that should be just fine for your needs. Unfortunately you need to refer to your motherboard manufacturer's support site to be certain your chosen memory will work correctly. Some memory will work at reduced speed and other memory will prevent the system from booting. Asus (again) has a neat trick called MemOK! on certain models that is a compatibility switch. With MemOK! enabled the system will run, and even if the speed is slower than you might like, you can at least confirm that your problem comes down to the memory.

Check your monitor connection

By this stage in the fault-finding game we hope you have a PC that is showing signs of life and the fans are turning. This can lead to the frustrating situation where your new gaming PC appears to be alive and well yet you cannot see anything on the screen.

There was a time when a monitor had a single cable to connect to your PC and that cable was hardwired at one end and had a simple connector at the other. These days you need to select a connection from an array that might include DisplayPort, HDMI, DVI and VGA. Quite a few graphics cards have as many as six outputs.

Once you have decided on the connection you want, plugged it into the graphics card and monitor and ensured the monitor has mains power, you should be ready for action. Turn on the monitor, turn on the PC and wait for the status LED to turn blue (or green, or whatever). Any decent monitor should automatically detect which input is being used so you need to be sure the monitor doesn't have any other inputs in use. However you might need to use the control buttons to manually select the correct input.

At this stage if you still don't have a picture showing on the monitor, there is something rather obvious that you need to check. These days Intel CPUs include a graphics core and so do certain series of AMD chips and this means you find graphics outputs on the I/O panel of many motherboards. If the BIOS is set to automatically select a graphics output then it shouldn't matter whether you connect to the I/O panel or graphics card, although obviously the integrated graphics will have much lower performance.

The problem comes when the BIOS is set to either use the IGP (Integrated Graphics Processor) or PCI Express output and you connect to the other output, which has been disabled. This will render the PC unusable until you swap from the disabled graphics to the correct set. Once you regain control of your PC you can use the BIOS set-up to enable whichever graphics outputs you want.

PART  Beep and error codes

If it all goes wrong and you still can't get your PC up and running then fear not, because many motherboards have features that can help you decipher precisely what the problem is. These only really occur when the problem is serious enough to prevent it from even booting up, so there aren't often too many to worry about. Here we're reprinting the beep and error codes from AMI and Award, makers of two very commonly used BIOS programs. But worry not if your codes are just a little too complicated to decipher – such as those from Phoenix – because there's always a resource online you can hunt down to discover the solution.

The feared Windows 'Blue Screen of Death' is far less common than it used to be.

```
A problem has been detected and windows has been shut down to prevent damage
to your computer.

DRIVER_IRQL_NOT_LESS_OR_EQUAL

If this is the first time you've seen this stop error screen,
restart your computer, If this screen appears again, follow
these steps:

Check to make sure any new hardware or software is properly installed.
If this is a new installation, ask your hardware or software manufacturer
for any windows updates you might need.

If problems continue, disable or remove any newly installed hardware
or software. Disable BIOS memory options such as caching or shadowing.
If you need to use Safe Mode to remove or disable components, restart
your computer, press F8 to select Advanced Startup Options, and then
select Safe Mode.

Technical information:

*** STOP: 0x000000D1 (0x0000000C,0x00000002,0x00000000,0xF86B5A89)

***          gv3.sys - Address F86B5A89 base at F86B5000, DateStamp 3dd991eb

Beginning dump of physical memory
Physical memory dump complete.
Contact your system administrator or technical support group for further
assistance.
```

AMI BIOS beep codes

Number of Beeps	Problem	Action
1 short	Memory refresh timer error.	Remove each memory module, clean the connecting edge that plugs into the motherboard socket, and replace. If that doesn't work, try restarting with a single memory module and see if you can identify the culprit by a process of elimination. If you still get the error code, replace with known good modules.
2 short	Parity error.	As with 1 beep above.
3 short	Main memory read/write test error.	As with 1 beep above.
4 short	Motherboard timer not operational.	Either the motherboard is faulty or one of the expansion cards has a problem. Remove all cards except the video card and restart. If the motherboard still issues this beep code, it has a serious, probably fatal problem. If the beeps stop, replace the cards one at a time and restart each time. This should identify the guilty party.
5 short	Processor error.	As with 4 beeps above.
6 short	Keyboard controller BAT test error.	As with 4 beeps above.
7 short	General exception error.	As with 4 beeps above.
8 short	Display memory error.	The video card is missing, faulty or incorrectly installed. Remove, clean the connecting contacts and replace. If that doesn't work, try using a different video card. If you are using integrated video instead of a video card, the motherboard may be faulty.
9 short	ROM checksum error.	As with 4 beeps above.
10 short	CMOS shutdown register read/write error.	As with 4 beeps above.
11 short	Cache memory bad.	As with 4 beeps above.
1 long, 2 short	Failure in video system.	A fault with the video BIOS ROM has occurred. Uninstall the graphics card and use the on-board graphics to find out if your GPU is the one causing the fault.
1 long, 3 short	Memory test failure.	There's an issue with your system memory; reinstall the RAM. If it is still faulty, try running the PC on a single stick of RAM (alternating between different sticks if the fault still occurs).
1 long, 8 short	Display test failure.	A fault with your video card – either your own GPU or on-board graphics on the motherboard – or its memory. The system will boot without it, but it means there's likelly a hardware fault with your video card.

AMIBIOS8 Checkpoint and Beep Code List version 1.2. Copyright of American Megatrends, Inc. Reprinted with permission. All rights reserved.

AMI BIOS error codes Here are some examples of onscreen error messages:

Error	Action
Gate20 Error	The BIOS is unable to properly control the motherboard's Gate A20 function, which controls access of memory over 1MB. This may indicate a problem with the motherboard.
Multi-Bit ECC Error	This message will only occur on systems using ECC-enabled memory modules. ECC memory has the ability to correct single-bit errors that may occur from faulty memory modules. A multiple bit corruption of memory has occurred, and the ECC memory algorithm cannot correct it. This may indicate a defective memory module.
Parity Error	Fatal Memory Parity Error. System halts after displaying this message.
Boot Failure	This is a generic message indicating the BIOS could not boot from a particular device. This message is usually followed by other information concerning the device.
Invalid Boot Diskette	A diskette was found in the drive, but it is not configured as a bootable diskette.

AMI BIOS error codes continued:

Error	Action
Drive Not Ready	The BIOS was unable to access the drive because it indicated it was not ready for data transfer. This is often reported by drives when no media is present.
A: Drive Error	The BIOS attempted to configure the A: drive during POST, but was unable to properly configure the device. This may be because of a bad cable or faulty diskette drive.
Insert BOOT diskette in A:	The BIOS attempted to boot from the A: drive, but could not find a proper boot diskette.
Reboot and Select proper Boot device or Insert Boot Media in selected Boot device	BIOS could not find a bootable device in the system and/or removable media drive does not contain media.
NO ROM BASIC	This message occurs on some systems when no bootable device can be detected.
Primary Master Hard Disk Error	The IDE/ATAPI device configured as Primary Master could not be properly initialized by the BIOS. This message is typically displayed when the BIOS is trying to detect and configure IDE/ATAPI devices in POST.
Primary Slave Hard Disk Error	The IDE/ATAPI device configured as Primary Slave could not be properly initialized by the BIOS. This message is typically displayed when the BIOS is trying to detect and configure IDE/ATAPI devices in POST.
Secondary Master Hard Disk Error	The IDE/ATAPI device configured as Secondary Master could not be properly initialized by the BIOS. This message is typically displayed when the BIOS is trying to detect and configure IDE/ATAPI devices in POST.
Secondary Slave Hard Disk Error	The IDE/ATAPI device configured as Secondary Slave could not be properly initialized by the BIOS. This message is typically displayed when the BIOS is trying to detect and configure IDE/ATAPI devices in POST.
Primary Master Drive – ATAPI Incompatible	The IDE/ATAPI device configured as Primary Master failed an ATAPI compatibility test. This message is typically displayed when the BIOS is trying to detect and configure IDE/ATAPI devices in POST.
Primary Slave Drive – ATAPI Incompatible	The IDE/ATAPI device configured as Primary Slave failed an ATAPI compatibility test. This message is typically displayed when the BIOS is trying to detect and configure IDE/ATAPI devices in POST.
Secondary Master Drive – ATAPI Incompatible	The IDE/ATAPI device configured as Secondary Master failed an ATAPI compatibility test. This message is typically displayed when the BIOS is trying to detect and configure IDE/ATAPI devices in POST.
Secondary Slave Drive – ATAPI Incompatible	The IDE/ATAPI device configured as Secondary Slave failed an ATAPI compatibility test. This message is typically displayed when the BIOS is trying to detect and configure IDE/ATAPI devices in POST.
S.M.A.R.T. Capable but Command Failed	The BIOS tried to send a S.M.A.R.T. message to a hard disk, but the command transaction failed. This message can be reported by an ATAPI device using the S.M.A.R.T. error reporting standard. S.M.A.R.T. failure messages may indicate the need to replace the hard disk.
S.M.A.R.T. Command Failed	The BIOS tried to send a S.M.A.R.T. message to a hard disk, but the command transaction failed. This message can be reported by an ATAPI device using the S.M.A.R.T. error reporting standard. S.M.A.R.T. failure messages may indicate the need to replace the hard disk.
S.M.A.R.T. Status BAD, Backup and Replace	A S.M.A.R.T. capable hard disk sends this message when it detects an imminent failure. This message can be reported by an ATAPI device using the S.M.A.R.T. error reporting standard. S.M.A.R.T. failure messages may indicate the need to replace the hard disk.
S.M.A.R.T. Capable and Status BAD	A S.M.A.R.T. capable hard disk sends this message when it detects an imminent failure. This message can be reported by an ATAPI device using the S.M.A.R.T. error reporting standard. S.M.A.R.T. failure messages may indicate the need to replace the hard disk.

AMI BIOS error codes continued:

Error	Action
BootSector Write!!	The BIOS has detected software attempting to write to a drive's boot sector. This is flagged as possible virus activity. This message will only be displayed if Virus Detection is enabled in AMIBIOS Setup.
VIRUS: Continue (Y/N)?	If the BIOS detects possible virus activity, it will prompt the user. This message will only be displayed if Virus Detection is enabled in AMIBIOS Setup.
DMA-2 Error	Error initializing secondary DMA controller. This is a fatal error, often indicating a problem with system hardware.
DMA Controller Error	POST error while trying to initialize the DMA controller. This is a fatal error, often indicating a problem with system hardware.
CMOS Date/Time Not Set	The CMOS Date and/or Time are invalid. This error can be resolved by readjusting the system time in AMIBIOS Setup.
CMOS Battery Low	CMOS Battery is low. This message usually indicates that the CMOS battery needs to be replaced. It could also appear when the user intentionally discharges the CMOS battery.
CMOS Settings Wrong	CMOS settings are invalid. This error can be resolved by using AMIBIOS Setup.
CMOS Checksum Bad	CMOS contents failed the Checksum check. Indicates that the CMOS data has been changed by a program other than the BIOS or that the CMOS is not retaining its data due to malfunction. This error can typically be resolved by using AMIBIOS Setup.
Keyboard Error	Keyboard is not present or the hardware is not responding when the keyboard controller is initialized.
Keyboard/Interface Error	Keyboard Controller failure. This may indicate a problem with system hardware.
System Halted	The system has been halted. A reset or power cycle is required to reboot the machine. This message appears after a fatal error has been detected.

Award BIOS beep codes

Number of Beeps	Problem	Action
1 long beep followed by 2 short beeps	Video card problem	Remove the card, clean the connecting edge that plugs into the motherboard socket, and replace. If that doesn't work, try an alternative video card to establish whether the problem lies with the card or the AGP slot. If you are using integrated video instead of a video card, the motherboard may be faulty.
Any other beeps	Memory problem	Remove each memory module, clean the connecting edge that plugs into the motherboard socket, and replace. If that doesn't work, try restarting with a single memory module and see if you can identify the culprit by a process of elimination. If you still get the error code, replace with known good modules.
1 long, 3 short	No detectable video card, or bad video card memory.	Ensure video card is correctly installed and powered. If it still occurs, there is a fault with the video card's memory
High frequency beeps while running	Overheating CPU.	A sign that your CPU is not being cooled properly. First check the cooling systems are powered and functioning. If problems persist, first replace thermal paste and – if still occurring – install more efficient cooling systems.
Repeating high/low beeps	Fault with CPU.	Check that the CPU is seated properly in its socket. If it is, the CPU may be damaged. This may also occur if the CPU's heat is too much, follow above resolutions.

Award BIOS error codes

Here are the standard Award onscreen error messages:

Error	Action
BIOS ROM checksum error – System halted	The checksum of the BIOS code in the BIOS chip is incorrect, indicating the BIOS code may have become corrupt. Contact your system dealer to replace the BIOS.
CMOS battery failed	The CMOS battery is no longer functional. Contact your system dealer for a replacement battery.
CMOS checksum error – Defaults loaded	Checksum of CMOS is incorrect, so the system loads the default equipment configuration. A checksum error may indicate that CMOS has become corrupt. This error may have been caused by a weak battery. Check the battery and replace if necessary.
CPU at nnnn	Displays the running speed of the CPU.
Display switch is set incorrectly	The display switch on the motherboard can be set to either monochrome or colour. This message indicates the switch is set to a different setting from that indicated in Setup. Determine which setting is correct, and then either turn off the system and change the jumper, or enter Setup and change the VIDEO selection.
Press ESC to skip memory test	The user may press Esc to skip the full memory test.
Floppy disk(s) fail	Cannot find or initialize the floppy drive controller or the drive. Make sure the controller is installed correctly. If no floppy drives are installed, be sure the Diskette Drive selection in Setup is set to NONE or AUTO.
HARD DISK initializing. Please wait a moment.	Some hard drives require extra time to initialize.
HARD DISK INSTALL FAILURE	Cannot find or initialize the hard drive controller or the drive. Make sure the controller is installed correctly. If no hard drives are installed, be sure the Hard Drive selection in Setup is set to NONE.
Hard disk(s) diagnosis fail	The system may run specific disk diagnostic routines. This message appears if one or more hard disks return an error when the diagnostics run.
Keyboard error or no keyboard present	Cannot initialize the keyboard. Make sure the keyboard is attached correctly and no keys are pressed during POST. To purposely configure the system without a keyboard, set the error halt condition in Setup to HALT ON ALL, BUT KEYBOARD. The BIOS then ignores the missing keyboard during POST.
Keyboard is locked out – Unlock the key	This message usually indicates that one or more keys have been pressed during the keyboard tests. Be sure no objects are resting on the keyboard.
Memory Test	This message displays during a full memory test, counting down the memory areas being tested.
Memory test fail	If POST detects an error during memory testing, additional information appears giving specifics about the type and location of the memory error.
Override enabled – Defaults loaded	If the system cannot boot using the current CMOS configuration, the BIOS can override the current configuration with a set of BIOS defaults designed for the most stable, minimal-performance system operations.
Press TAB to show POST screen	System OEMs may replace the Phoenix Technologies' AwardBIOS POST display with their own proprietary display. Including this message in the OEM display permits the operator to switch between the OEM display and the default POST display.
Primary master hard disk fail	POST detects an error in the primary master IDE hard drive.
Primary slave hard disk fail	POST detects an error in the primary slave IDE hard drive.
Secondary master hard disk fail	POST detects an error in the secondary master IDE hard drive.
Secondary slave hard disk fail	POST detects an error in the secondary slave IDE hard drive.

Index